D0906301

# HELLO, HABITS

ALSO BY FUMIO SASAKI

*Goodbye, Things: The New Japanese Minimalism*

# HELLO, HABITS

## A Minimalist's Guide to a Better Life

## Fumio Sasaki

### Translated by Eriko Sugita

**W. W. NORTON & COMPANY**
*Independent Publishers Since 1923*

BOKUTACHI WA SHUUKAN DE, DEKITEIRU.
Copyright © 2021, 2018 by Fumio Sasaki
English translation rights arranged with WANI BOOKS CO., LTD.
through Japan UNI Agency, Inc., Tokyo

For information about permission to reproduce selections from this book, write to
Permissions, W. W. Norton & Company, Inc., 500 Fifth Avenue, New York, NY 10110

For information about special discounts for bulk purchases, please contact
W. W. Norton Special Sales at specialsales@wwnorton.com or 800-233-4830

Manufacturing by Lake Book Manufacturing
Production manager: Anna Oler

Library of Congress Cataloging-in-Publication Data

Names: Sasaki, Fumio, 1979– author.
Title: Hello, habits : a minimalist's guide to a better life / by Fumio Sasaki ; translated
    by Eriko Sugita.
Other titles: Bokutachi wa shūkan de dekiteiru. English
Description: New York, NY : W.W. Norton & Company, [2021]
Identifiers: LCCN 2020035372 | ISBN 9781324005582 (cloth) |
    ISBN 9781324005599 (epub)
Subjects: LCSH: Habit. | Learning, Psychology of. | Self-management (Psychology)
Classification: LCC BF335 .S18513 2021 | DDC 179/.9—dc23
LC record available at https://lccn.loc.gov/2020035372

W. W. Norton & Company, Inc., 500 Fifth Avenue, New York, N.Y. 10110
www.wwnorton.com

W. W. Norton & Company Ltd., 15 Carlisle Street, London W1D 3BS

1 2 3 4 5 6 7 8 9 0

# CONTENTS

# INTRODUCTION

I always thought that I had no talent.

I could never continue to do something for an extended period no matter what I tried, and I was unable to produce significant results in either my studies or sports. But since I started to study habits, I've changed my mind. It's not a major issue whether or not I have talent.

Because talent isn't something that's "given" to us; it's "made," as a result of a continuation of habits.

There is an author that I like by the name of Kyohei Sakaguchi. His novels are written with combinations of words that are completely different from other authors'. And he can write moving melodies on his guitar, and his illustrations rival those by contemporary artists. He has recently been making chairs and even knitting. No matter how you look at him, he appears gifted.

But I heard that even this man had been told by his father, "You don't have talent, so give it up," while his brother would say, "You've just been lucky with flukes from the number of attempts you've been making." There's a phrase that Sakaguchi repeats like a mantra: "It isn't talent. It's continuing." I hear that even baseball star Ichiro and internationally best-selling author Haruki Murakami—and for that matter, anyone else who thrives in whatever it is that they do—generally don't acknowledge that they are gifted.

On the other hand, stories about gifted people captivate us: *Dragon Ball*, in which talent is awakened by anger; *Slam Dunk*, in which the protagonist, who has so far only been getting into fights, suddenly shows off a magnificent jump; and Hollywood films like *The Matrix*, in which a "chosen one" all of a sudden becomes aware of his capabilities.

When you live a real life for a while, you begin to realize that talent is somewhat different from these types of things. Look at the gifted individuals in the world; you'll see that they are all making proper efforts. There's a line that goes like this:

*Genius is often only the power of making continuous efforts.*
—Elbert Hubbard

Okay, I get it. Perhaps "genius" refers to a person who can continue to make efforts. But then, I thought: Maybe I don't have "the talent to continue to make efforts."

My feeling now is that words like "talent" and "effort" are being used under a misconception. Talent isn't something given to us by the heavens, and effort doesn't mean work so strenuous that we have to grit our teeth. I think the concept of "habits" can bring talent and effort back to the normal people out there. These are not things that may only be achieved by a limited few; they are things that we can all acquire, depending on how we go about it. In brief:

- Talent isn't something that you're "given"; it's something that's "created" after you make an effort.
- These efforts can be maintained if you turn them into habits.
- The methods for these habits are something that you can learn.

Writing my previous work, *Goodbye, Things*, freed me from my inferiority complex over money and possessions. And in writing this book, I am trying to relieve myself of my complex over "effort" and "talent."

I think this is going to turn out to be the last "self-help" book for me.

Let us begin our final preparations.

## How to Read This Book

The composition of this book is the same as when you're acquiring a habit: the beginning is the hardest part. So, if you want to quickly learn the "tips for making things a habit," you can go ahead and read just Chapter 3.

In Chapter 1, we consider the issue of "willpower." It often happens that we want to acquire some type of habit but end up being unable to persevere. And we often say, "I have a weak will." I will consider what exactly this willpower is that we express as being strong or weak.

In Chapter 2, I look at what habits are, as well as the issue of "awareness." This is because I consider habits to be "actions that we take without much thought"—in other words, they are actions that we take without calling up our "awareness," which we believe to be our mind.

In Chapter 3, I explain in stages the steps for actually acquiring habits, breaking them down into fifty parts. These are points that will serve as references when you start or quit doing something. While there are many books on habits, my intention has been to compile their essence in a single book.

In Chapter 4, I rewrite the meanings of the words "talent" and "effort" to capture what has become clear to me by studying habits, and the expanded possibilities of habits that I have witnessed by putting them into practice. Habits are not only effective for achieving objectives; I feel that they have deeper meaning.

*Habit is as second nature.*
—Cicero

*Habit a second nature! Habit is ten times nature.*
—The Duke of Wellington

*We are what we repeatedly do. Excellence, then,*
*is not an act, but a habit.*
—Will Durant

# HELLO, HABITS

# CHAPTER 1

# WHAT IS WILLPOWER?

## How I spend my days

"I'm exactly the type of person I wanted to be." My favorite film director, Clint Eastwood, once said something cool like that.

There's no way I could ever say that. But I am spending the types of days that I used to want to spend. I'd like to give you a look at an average day in my life.

---

## MY SCHEDULE ON A TYPICAL DAY

| | |
|---|---|
| 5 a.m. | Get up > do some yoga. |
| 5:30 a.m. | Meditate. |
| 6:00 a.m. | Work on my writing or my blog. |
| 7 a.m. | Clean house > take a shower > do the laundry > have breakfast > prepare my lunch. |
| 8 a.m. | Write in my diary > practice English > read the news or social media. |
| 9:10 a.m. | Take a power nap (a strategic way to go back to bed). |
| 9:30 a.m. | "Commute" to the library. |
| 11:30 a.m. | Eat lunch. |
| 2:30 p.m. | Leave the library. |
| 3 p.m. | Take a power nap. |
| 3:30 p.m. | Go to the gym. |
| 5:30 p.m. | Shop for groceries at the supermarket, return emails and check social media. |
| 6 p.m. | Watch a movie after dinner. |
| 9 p.m. | Bring out my yoga mat and stretch. |
| 9:30 p.m. | Go to bed. |

---

My schedule is basically the same each day, and it doesn't change whether it's the weekend or a holiday. My off days are when I have special plans like seeing friends, going to events, or traveling. I take about a day off each week. I'm now thirty-eight and single. I live alone, and I write as an occupation.

"Anyone can do that if they're single and they have freedom as a freelancer," you may think. But things were completely different for me when I first obtained the time and freedom that I had dreamed of.

## Enjoying retirement for a while

> *All of humanity's problems stem from man's inability to sit quietly in a room alone.*
>
> —Blaise Pascal

In 2016, I left the publishing company where I worked and began writing freelance. As I had just received a bonus I wouldn't have to worry about money for a while. No one would get mad at me no matter how much I slept each day, and I was free to go out and frolic during business hours. I had spent twelve busy years working as an editor. It wouldn't hurt to take it easy for a while. That's what I thought.

So, I took up diving, surfing, marathon running, taking on many challenges that had been on my bucket list. There are many new skills I've learned, too: driving a car, growing vegetables, and DIY work. I moved from Tokyo to Kyoto, and enjoyed visiting places I didn't know in the Kansai area.

This may appear to be an ideal situation. Many people would probably like to spend their time like this if they won the lottery or after they retire: not doing things you don't like doing, and doing everything you've ever wanted to do.

## We're happier if we don't have too much free time

When I was working as an editor, it had been a great joy to read books during the short breaks I had after eating lunch. I thought I'd have more time to enjoy myself if I quit work, but in reality, it wasn't like that. You don't tend to read when you have the whole day to read.

People often imagine that they "could do something if they had the time," but sometimes you can't if you have *too much* time on your hands.

It was also tough to find something to do each day. I'd come up with a chore and take care of it, and I'd find a place that looked interesting to visit and go there, but I would eventually get bored.

I ended up daydreaming more often. I would throw my abdominal release ball at the ceiling and catch it as it came back down. This was the only thing I had lately gotten good at doing. One time, I went to a nearby hot spring spa in the neighborhood in the afternoon—but then I realized that for some reason, I wasn't happy at all. It was no wonder—I had no stress or fatigue that needed to be healed.

According to a study conducted by the Japanese government, the level of our happiness is said to decrease when we have more than seven free hours in a day. I really agree. I think the conditions for happiness are the luxury of time and the freedom to do what you want. But being totally immersed in time and freedom isn't going to make you happy, either.

What awaited me after I escaped from a lack of freedom was the pain of freedom. Gandhi once said, "Indolence is a delightful but distressing state; we must be doing something to be happy." I feel the same way. There was delight, but it was very distressing. The vegetables I started planting wouldn't grow at all. I looked at those vegetables and thought they were kind of like me. This wasn't the way things were supposed to be.

People often say, "Let's just do the things that we like to do." That's a good idea. But it's completely different from "doing *only* the things that we like to do."

## A safety net called minimalism

What saved me was the fact that I was practicing a minimalist lifestyle. I had few things at home, and I had a habit of tidying up and cleaning house. There's a connection between the state of your mind and the state of your home. I think the fact that my place was always clean supported me like a safety net when I fell into depression. I'm really glad I reduced my possessions.

It was also good that I had already stopped drinking. If I hadn't, I think I would have started drinking in broad daylight to distract myself. What had been missing in me was a sense of achievement in my everyday life, feeling a sense of self-development. I should have known deep down. Playing hooky and staying away from school might make you happy if you can get away with it, but the pleasure will eventually wear off. More than once I felt tormented after thinking up some excuse and writing it on our schedule board and leaving the office.

I feel a strong sense of fate in the fact that I had chosen "habits" as my next theme to write about after minimalism. Without this theme, my mind might have gone back to my sloppy pre-minimalist days.

Of course, with my current habits, I take advantage of my position as a freelancer, and they wouldn't be possible if I had young children. But you can't acquire habits just because you have lots of time and energy, and in fact these things can sometimes turn out to be obstacles. I believe that the efforts I made and the things I learned in order to acquire habits will be useful in some way even to people who are busy with their work or raising children.

## Why do New Year's resolutions end up being failures?

All of mine have been failures.

- Getting up early in the morning and living an ordered life
- Maintaining a clean place to live
- Not overeating or drinking excessively and maintaining my proper weight
- Exercising regularly
- Getting started on my studies and my work instead of postponing things

Sleep, cleaning house, eating, exercising, studying, and work. The habits that we want to acquire are mostly the same for everyone. The problem lies in identifying why it's so tough to accomplish them.

I'm no exception. I've always continued to set objectives for the New Year. In one study, the probability of these targets being accomplished by the end of the year was a mere 8 percent. My objectives were always among the 92 percent that weren't fulfilled, and my "New Year's resolutions" never changed.

I always thought that it was because I had "weak willpower." "I have a weak will." Everyone says that when they can't accomplish something. It's a way of thinking that there are people in this world who have a strong will, and those who have a weak will.

It's this "willpower" that I'd like to consider. Although it might get a little complicated, I'd like to give detailed consideration to this willpower that everyone mentions, without really knowing too much about what it is and how it works.

Why is it so tough to acquire habits in the first place? It's because there are contradictions between the "rewards" that we see in front of us and the "rewards" in the future.

## Everything is based on "reward" and "punishment"

As the ideas of "reward" and "punishment" are indispensable themes for habits, I'd like to sort through them in advance.

- Eating good food
- Getting plenty of sleep
- Earning money
- Interacting with your favorite people and peers
- Getting "likes" on social media

All of these are rewards. You can simply consider them "things that make you feel good."

We can consider that all human actions are taken looking for some type of reward. The problem is that there are sometimes contradictions.

It's a reward to eat the sweets set in front of you. It's also a reward to make an effort not to eat them, and to get healthy or enhance your figure instead. We can say that gaining weight or getting sick as a result of eating too much are punishments. It means that if we keep enjoying the rewards in front of us, we'll not only be unable to obtain rewards in the future, but will also end up getting punished someday.

We know the types of actions we're supposed to take:

- Losing weight by making an effort not to eat
- Exercising instead of lying around
- Getting up early in the morning instead of staying up late engaging in some pastime
- Getting to our work or studies instead of playing games or using our smartphones

But it isn't all that easy. We know we'll be able to get ready to go out in the morning at a leisurely pace and board the train before rush hour (a reward) if we get up early, but we can't overcome the temptation of staying in bed for five more minutes (a reward), and keep hitting the snooze button. Even when we know that "This is booze that will give me a hangover!" (a punishment), we can't stop drinking from the bottle of wine in our hand (a reward). We're aware that waiting to get started on our work or our homework will result in getting frantic (a punishment) later on, yet we can't help getting wrapped up in a game or our smartphone (a reward).

The reason why we can't acquire good habits is because we often surrender to the reward in front of us. People who can overcome the rewards flashing in front of their eyes in order to win rewards in the future or avoid punishment are sometimes called "people with strong willpower."

## An apple today or two apples tomorrow?

What if Billy came home from school one day and his mom said to him:

"Hi Billy. You can have a cake a year from now if you do your homework before you go out to play."

Wouldn't Billy—or anyone else for that matter—head straight to the field where his friend is waiting for him?

It isn't easy for people to imagine future rewards. So, they tend to see the value of, and choose, rewards that are in front of them instead of those that await them in the future. It was apples that Richard Thaler, a theorist in behavioral economics, used in an experiment to consider this issue. I would like you to think about which of the following choices you would make.

Question 1
   Would you rather:
       A. Receive an apple a year from today
       B. Receive two apples a year and a day from today

The majority of people who were asked this chose B. They will have had to wait a whole year; another day won't make them suffer. They chose to obtain two apples. However . . .

Question 2
　　Would you rather:
　　　　A. Receive an apple today
　　　　B. Receive two apples tomorrow

In this case, many people, even those who chose B as their previous choice, choose A. The necessary action of waiting an additional day to receive an additional apple, and the reward for waiting, are exactly the same, but for some reason, the responses change.

Some people may not like apples; not everyone is as attracted to apples as Adam was. So an experiment was also conducted using money, which everyone should like.

Question 3
　　Would you rather:
　　　　A. Receive cash on Friday (for example, receive $10)
　　　　B. Receive 25 percent more cash on Monday (i.e., three days later) (for example, receive $12.50)

The interesting thing is that when asked before Friday, most people would rationally choose B, but when they're asked on Friday, 60 percent change their minds and choose the lesser amount in front of them. Maybe you'll choose B when you're calm-headed, like when you're reading this book. But what if a ten-dollar bill is being waved in front of you?

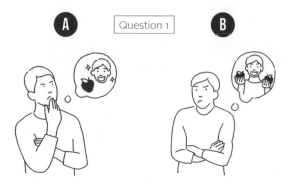

Receive an apple a year from today    Receive two apples a year and a day from today

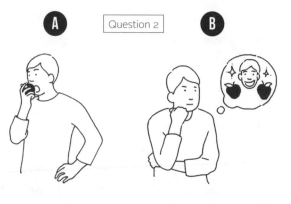

Receive an apple today    Receive two apples tomorrow

It's hard to visualize an apple that you'll be receiving a year from now, and it doesn't really seem to concern you, so you choose the response with the extra day of waiting. The more distant a reward may be in the future, the less value it seems to have. This doesn't only apply to rewards. The same thing can be said for punishment. You'll be pressured right before your exams if you don't start studying early, but at that earlier point, you can't imagine how you'll feel in the future.

You might develop lung cancer if you smoke, and you might become diabetic if you continue to eat sweets, but punishment in the future tends to be looked at lightly. It means there's greater value in the nicotine or sugars that are now in front of you.

## A pressing desire to have the reward in front of us

In these ways, people tend to overestimate the rewards in front of them and underestimate the rewards and punishments that exist in the future. In behavioral economics, this is called "hyperbolic discounting." People can't rationally evaluate value like a computer. We want to eat an apple that's set in front of us right now, and we want $10 now rather than $12.50 three days from now. We can't wait.

And when the reward is a great distance away, we can't get in the mood to do something. It isn't as if refraining from eating the tasty dish in front of us or running today will allow us to lose a couple of pounds tomorrow. It might take a month or three months to lose those pounds.

Hyperbolic discounting can explain why it's hard for us to acquire good habits like dieting, exercising, living an orderly life, or getting right to work.

## Why can't we wait for a reward in the future?

Why is it, then, that people follow an annoying practice like hyperbolic discounting? It's because there still isn't a big difference between the workings of people who lived in ancient times, hunting and gathering, and people who live today. Human civilization is only around five thousand years old, and that's only 0.2 percent of the history of humans. So, 99 percent of human development in body and mind has been in service of hunting and gathering. It takes tens of thousands of years for a species to evolve. We're still unconsciously deploying strategies that were effective during ancient times.

What was necessary to live at that time had to have been, above all, to obtain food. When you didn't know when the next time would be that you would have access to food, it must have been an effective strategy to eat food as soon as you found it.

The situation is completely different today. In an advanced country like Japan, most people don't have trouble feeding themselves. There's more than enough delicious, high-calorie food at supermarkets and convenience stores. What's necessary now is to avoid that type of temptation as much as possible and to exercise in order to use up your extra calories. That's become a new secret for staying healthy and living a long life.

What should really be the most efficient way to live well is to take in only the necessary amount of calories, and then sleep like a cat. But unlike cats, humans have created a society where they can't survive by simply sleeping all the time. The work that's done by each human being has become highly sophisticated, which has made it necessary to endure boring studies and to take difficult exams to receive credentials, which give us an edge in our work and allow us to make large sums of money.

Men who lived during a period when they could be attacked and killed by a carnivore the next day probably didn't have the time to enjoy romance or live it up as a bachelor. I'm sure they would have gone straight to sex and producing offspring when they found a woman who was willing to accept them. But men like that probably wouldn't be accepted today.

The rules of the game played by society have changed to not jumping to grab the rewards in front of you but instead obtaining the rewards further on down the line, yet the nature of the players hasn't changed. That's why annoying phenomena like hyperbolic discounting occur.

## Children who are somehow able to wait for marshmallows

Still, there are some people who can quickly adapt to the rules of such new games. They're the ones with the "strong willpower" who can maintain good habits and make efforts to achieve their objectives. What's the difference between people who give in to the rewards in front of them and those who can wait for rewards in the future?

An answer lies in the famous "marshmallow test" conducted by psychologist Walter Mischel concerning this issue. I would like you to pay attention to this marshmallow test, as it will be one of the central themes in this book.

This test was conducted on children aged four to five at Stanford University's Bing Nursery School during the 1960s. First, children chose what they wanted to eat the most from among snacks like marshmallows, cookies, and pretzels. One of those snacks (I'll use marshmallows here as an example) is placed on the table where a child is seated. He or she is then prompted to choose from the following. It's really a simple experiment.

A. Eat the marshmallow in front of them right now.
B. Do not eat the marshmallow and wait for a maximum of twenty minutes for the researcher to come back. Receive two marshmallows if they can wait.

A bell is placed near the marshmallow. The children can ring it and eat the marshmallow if they can't wait. The children will receive two marshmallows as a reward if they can refrain from leaving the table or eating the marshmallow before the researcher comes back.

What's important about this test is that it encapsulates the skill to forgo the temptation of the reward in front of them to obtain a bigger reward in the future, which is necessary for forming good habits.

The children sniff at the marshmallow dreamily, pretend to bite it, or lick the powder from the marshmallow on their hands as they wait. The majority of children who continued to stare at the marshmallows failed to not eat it. Once they allowed themselves to take just a bite, it wasn't possible for them to stop. They were no different from adults in the way they placed their hands on their cheeks and suffered as they faced the dilemma of not being able to eat when they wanted to.

In the test, the children were able to wait for an average of six minutes, and two-thirds of them were unable to wait and ended up eating the marshmallow in front of them. The remaining third were able to wait, and obtained two marshmallows.

## Can we predict the future with the marshmallow test?

This experiment starts to get interesting from here. A surprising result of long-term follow-up studies on the children who took the marshmallow test was that the longer they were able to wait when they took the test as preschoolers, the better they did on their SATs.

Children who had been able to wait for fifteen minutes scored better than those who failed in thirty seconds by 210 points.

Children who had been able to wait for their marshmallows were liked more by their peers and their teachers and obtained higher-paying jobs. They didn't become obese when they became middle-aged, their body mass index (BMI) was lower on average, and their risks of drug abuse were low as well. It's scary that a test taken when people were four or five years old could predict the type of life that they would have in decades to follow.

A study conducted on a thousand New Zealanders from the time of their birth to the age of thirty-two yielded similar results, showing that children who had higher rates of self-control at an early age demonstrated lower rates of obesity as adults, fewer sexually transmitted diseases, and better dental and overall health.

## Questions that arise from the marshmallow test

The first thing that comes to mind when you look at these results is this: "Okay, okay. So it's decided from birth whether a child has the capacity to obtain rewards in the future without grabbing the rewards in front of them. I now know why I can't acquire good habits. Fine." And you give up. But in contrast to the clear results, I think it's an experiment that generates various questions. Here are two that I came up with:

1.  The children who were able to wait used something like "willpower" to forgo the temptation of the marshmallows in front of them. How does such willpower work, if it exists? (If it's true that good habits are acquired because of "strong willpower" like everyone says, then an understanding of willpower should deepen our understanding of habits.)
2.  Is that "willpower" already determined at the age of four or five? Isn't it possible to acquire willpower later on?

## The radish test: Will our willpower be reduced if we use it?

First, I'd like to think about question 1. How does this "willpower" that some of the children seem to have used to forgo the temptation in front of them, work?

The "radish test" is the most famous test in considering the issue of "willpower." It's an experiment that psychologist Roy Baumeister conducted using chocolate chip cookies and radishes.

A group of hungry college students were made to sit at a table set with cookies and a bowl of radishes. The room was filled with the sweet smell of fresh-baked cookies.

The students were divided into three groups:

A. Students who were allowed to eat the chocolate chip cookies
B. Students who were only allowed to eat the raw radishes
C. Students who were not allowed to eat anything and had to remain hungry

The poor subjects in group B were told that because the cookies were being used in the next experiment, they could only eat the radishes. Although none ate the cookies, it was clear that they were attracted to the cookies as they sniffed at their aroma or picked them up and accidentally dropped them on the floor.

Next, the students were instructed to solve a puzzle in a separate room. Cruelly, these puzzles were set up so that they couldn't be solved. The students were being tested not on their intelligence or ability to solve puzzles, but in order to see how long it would take them to give up on the tough challenge.

The students in group A who ate the cookies and those in group C who didn't eat anything were able to work on the puzzles for an average of twenty minutes. The students in group B were only able to work on them for an average of eight minutes before giving up.

For a long time, this experiment was interpreted as follows: The students in the group that had only been able to eat radishes had already used up a considerable amount of their willpower by refraining from eating the cookies, and that was why they gave up the difficult puzzle that required willpower. In other words, willpower was like a limited resource, and the more it was used, the less of it there was.

It's easy to imagine from this example that willpower is limited. Perhaps we can imagine it as spiritual strength that has limitations, something like the MPs (magic points) that are required to use magic in an RPG (role-playing game). If you aren't familiar with RPGs, you can simply think of it as gasoline in the fuel tank of a car. When you drive your car, the amount of gasoline in the fuel tank decreases.

This seems to perfectly explain the actions that we can't help taking in our daily lives.

If we continue to work overtime at work, we stop by a convenience store on our way home and buy sweets or drink lots of alcohol. In that state, we get short-tempered over the smallest actions by someone else.

In one experiment, students who were stressed wouldn't exercise, their consumption of cigarettes and junk food increased, and they got lazy in brushing their teeth or shaving. They were also sleeping in more and making impulsive purchases.

These types of things are probably familiar occurrences for anyone. They happen all too often to me, anyway. Willpower really does seem to be something that becomes "reduced." No one can continue to make complicated calculations or engage in difficult creative work over long periods. Energy really does become depleted at some point, and it becomes necessary for us to rest or to get some sleep.

## Willpower isn't something that is easily reduced

Given those examples, some people thought, "Isn't willpower simply a matter of your blood sugar level?" This hypothesis was checked using "real lemonade" sweetened with sugar and "fake lemonade" made with artificial sweetener. The blood sugar level didn't increase for the subjects who were made to drink fake lemonade, and they didn't continue the test. Everyone knows that you won't feel like doing anything if you're too hungry.

Is it okay to consider willpower simply as an issue of blood sugar levels and energy being reduced when you use it? I don't think so, because there are too many things that can't be explained with these experiments alone.

For example, there are several entries in my diary of "Eating ramen noodles > ended up eating potato chips, too > also ate ice cream to top it off." It's like, I've already eaten ramen noodles, so it doesn't make any difference whether I go ahead and eat potato chips and ice cream, too! And that's how we eat and drink too much.

Since I didn't force myself to refrain from eating ramen or potato chips, I shouldn't have had to use my willpower, and my blood sugar level should have fully recovered. Why hadn't I been able to use that willpower that I preserved and recovered to stay away from that ice cream?

We should be hungry and our willpower should have recovered after we've exercised at the gym. But even if I stop by a super-market on the way home, I don't feel like reaching for unhealthy foods. On the other hand, it's when I've been lazing around thinking that I should go to the gym but don't manage to do so that I reach for those sinful foods.

## There are types of willpower that will be reduced by "not taking action"

If willpower is like energy that's reduced when you use it, "pre-serving" it as much as possible should be an effective strategy. It's like Kaede Rukawa in *Slam Dunk* forfeiting the first half of a basketball game and concentrating in the second half.

But that would mean that you can use your willpower more effectively by sleeping in in the morning and always going to meetings at the last minute. Is there anyone who would see you slacking off in the morning who'd think, "Has he possibly . . . forfeited the morning?" People who slack off in the morning also tend to slack off in the afternoon.

Unless I get up properly in the morning, I am often unable to focus on my work after that or on my workout to follow. I have regrets about not doing what I should have done and sometimes can't proceed to whatever it is that I'm supposed to do next. In other words, willpower can be reduced not only by doing something, but also by "not doing" something.

## Willpower is affected by emotions

I believe it's emotions that we lose out on by "not doing something." Our blood sugar level will recover if we eat or drink too much, but the emotion of regretting will also be generated. It's the same when we're unable to acquire a habit that we've decided to acquire; we'll develop a lack of confidence in ourselves.

Various puzzles can be solved if we consider our emotions as a key factor. Towards the end of a marathon, we sometimes high-five the people who line the streets to cheer us on. Our knees hurt and we may feel that we've reached our limit, but exchanging a high-five with an excited child will give us the will to go on just a little longer. It's the recovery of our willpower.

There are variations of the lemonade test I mentioned earlier that go like this: Test subjects' willpower recovered right away when instead of drinking "real lemonade," they were made to spit it out right away. The lemonade that they only had in their mouths was probably something like a high-five.

It isn't as if it replenished their energy or sugar. It just seemed like a little treat that made them feel happy.

## Uncertainty will reduce our willpower

The emotion of joy that's generated when we put lemonade in our mouth or do a high-five will allow us to recover our willpower. Conversely, uncertainty and a lack of confidence are negative emotions that exhaust our willpower. And we fall into a vicious cycle of reduced willpower that leads to an inability to tackle the next challenge.

There was an experiment using serotonin that supports this. Serotonin balances our sympathetic and parasympathetic nerves and stabilizes our mind. People feel uncertainty if these aren't functioning properly. It's known that serotonin is inert in the brains of people who suffer from depression.

In an experiment in which the serotonin level in people's brains was temporarily increased and decreased, the subjects tried to take the rewards in front of them when their serotonin levels were low, though they tried to wait for future rewards when their serotonin levels were high. It means that low serotonin levels, or uncertainties, cause reductions in willpower and inhibit the achievement of good habits.

## It isn't willpower, but emotions, that can be spent

When we consider the radish test from such a perspective of emotions, it, too, can be seen in a different light. In front of you are chocolate chip cookies that smell good, but you're told that those aren't something that you can eat. Wouldn't you feel like you aren't being respected and simply become sad? Hadn't it actually been this emotion that was affected in the radish test, and not willpower?

There will be times when you're busy with your work and have simple meals consisting of items that you buy at a convenience store. You should have been able to preserve your willpower as you haven't done any complicated cooking, yet you're somehow left with a sense of melancholy. Isn't it because of the feeling that you aren't treating yourself well, rather than an issue with the flavor of the food? I think women are able to paint their nails and vigorously engage in making themselves beautiful, despite the need for willpower to do these tedious things, because they're boosting their self-esteem by taking care of themselves.

It's the same for me when I make an effort to clean up more often when I'm busy. People's homes get messy when they're busy, and that's because they tend to think, "I don't have the time to do something like that!" But my feeling is that it's actually more effective to tackle your tasks after cleaning house. Our willpower increases because we feel good that we've tidied up.

## We can wait for our marshmallows if we're feeling good

The results from the marshmallow test also varied depending on the emotions that people experienced at the time. Children who were told to "think of something fun while they wait" were able to wait three times longer. On the other hand, children who were told to think about something sad could no longer wait at all.

There's also an experiment conducted by psychologist Tim Edwards-Hart. He formed two groups and showed the subjects one of two films before putting them to work:

A.  A happy film
B.  A sad film

Work efficiency improved by more than 20 percent for the subjects in group A. It appears that it isn't just for show that the film company Pixar has a slide at their offices, or that the offices at Google are colorful, full of toys, and almost like a nursery school for adults.

## A hot system and a cool system

"Not doing" something will generate negative emotions and uncertainties, and it will also stop people from becoming motivated, which is another ongoing challenge. Why is it that such an awful vicious circle awaits us? In order to understand that, we need to take a look at our brain. The brain is structured like an onion, where the new parts that have been generated through evolution wrap around the old, primitive parts. And many researchers believe that the brain has two systems:

1.  Instinctive. It's reflexive, and the speed is fast; a system that determines things through emotions and intuition. Corresponds to the limbic system, the striatum, and the amygdala: the "old brain."
2.  Rational. The response speed is slower, and it won't work unless there's an awareness of something. A system that enables thinking, the imagination, and planning. Corresponds to the frontal lobe, or the "new brain."

While there are various names for these two systems, I would like to follow Walter Mischel from the marshmallow test and call them the following:

(1) the "hot system" and (2) the "cool system"

It's a little complicated, but I think it's easy to understand if you can envision the following types of images:

1.  The hot system is hot because you're driven by your emotions or desires ("Yay! A marshmallow! I'm going to eat it!").
2.  The cool system calmly analyzes and deals with something ("Okay, so I get a bigger reward later on if I don't eat this . . .").

With the hot system and the cool system, one won't function as strongly if the other is activated. They're constantly interacting with and supplementing each other.

## Stress can make the hot system can go wild

Our instinctive hot system becomes active when we feel negative or have uncertain thoughts. As I said earlier, a lot of our body systems are holdovers from ancient times.

The majority of the causes of stress at that time had to have been whether or not we could find food. So it must have been an effective way to cope with stress by eating the food in front of us, and resting whenever we could.

But today, we aren't going to be in a critical condition, like not being able to obtain food, just because we've felt a little stress at work. Yet our main strategies against stress remain unchanged.

Our instinct kicks in: It seems rational to take in more calories or to escape from things that we don't like. It's possible to explain the reason why we eat or drink too much or become unable to take on our next challenge in the following way:

## Cooling off using our cool system

Our cool system keeps our hot system from running wild.

Let me give you an example. Let's say that you're walking down the street on a rainy day, and a speeding car drives through a puddle and splashes you. Anyone is bound to get upset or shout at the driver. That's a response due to our hot system. But it can be controlled by our "cognition" or our "conscious mind," which is handled by our cool system. Cognition is to see reality not exactly as it stands, but to look at it in a somewhat different way.

"Maybe there was a pregnant woman in the car who had suddenly started having labor pains, and so they were rushing her to the hospital."

You can appease your anger when you think like that. Walter Mischel called this "cooling" the hot system. That's what it means for the cool system and the hot system to interact.

## Is willpower a talent that we're born with?

It's my second question that most concerns me with regard to the marshmallow test. Seeing as everything from a person's performance in school to his or her state of health could be predicted by the test results, the question is whether willpower is really determined by the age of four or five.

According to Mischel, the majority of the children who were able to wait fifteen minutes and receive two marshmallows demonstrated excellent willpower for decades to follow. But that's "the majority" of them, and there were also subjects whose abilities became reduced. There were also children who immediately ate their marshmallows who grew able to control themselves as they got older. It's something that gives us hope.

## Change your environment and your willpower will change

What I want you to be aware of is that when the criteria change, the results from the marshmallow test will change significantly:

- Subjects were able to wait twice as long when marshmallows were shown on a projector instead of using real marshmallows.
- Subjects who had not been able to wait could wait ten times longer when the marshmallows were hidden under a tray.

In other words, simply by removing the real marshmallows in front of them, the subjects were able to wait longer. The children who had been able to wait in the initial experiment sang, made funny faces, played the piano, or closed their eyes and went to sleep. They knew how to divert their thoughts from the marshmallows in front of them. On the other hand, the children who continued to stare at the marshmallows in front of them generally failed.

## Isn't it an issue of the number of times that they were seduced?

How about this: maybe the children who couldn't wait in the marshmallow test failed not because they had weak willpower, but because they were simply seduced more often by the marshmallows.

The children who couldn't wait and went ahead and ate the marshmallows right away had been staring at the sweets. It means they had been imagining the taste of the sweet, plump marshmallows over and over as they waited, and ended up being seduced.

And in fact, the children who were instructed to "think about the marshmallows as they waited" were only able to wait for short periods.

## Dopamine does bad things to us

Failure ensues when you continue to look at the marshmallows.

This is because of the "bad things" that dopamine does to us.

The general understanding of dopamine is that it's a neurotransmitter that's released when we experience a pleasant sensation. It's released when we eat something tasty, obtain money, or have sex with the person that we love. That's why people take action to seek those pleasures. That's one way to explain what it is, but the mechanism of dopamine is a little more complicated.

Neurologist Wolfram Schultz conducted an experiment in which he gave various rewards to monkeys. The striatum, the part of the brain where dopamine is concentrated, rapidly fired when a drop of fruit juice was dropped on the monkeys' tongues.

But when light signals were shown to the monkeys before they were given the juice, the dopamine began to be released not in response to the juice, but rather to the light. Dopamine began to correspond not to the action itself, but rather to the "sign" of what to expect.

It's the same with people, and I think it applies to various cases.

Don't people get most excited about social media like Facebook or Twitter not when they're checking their messages, but when they receive a notification?

Don't we most feel like drinking beer not because we're attracted to the beer itself, but when we're seduced by the sounds of a can being popped open or the *chug-chug* of it being poured into a glass?

Consider also the following experiment: when rats are given a drug that obstructs dopamine, they won't eat, and they'll starve to death. Because the desire for something doesn't occur when dopamine is obstructed, the rats didn't attempt to eat, no matter how hungry they were or what tasty foods were available in front of them.

In this way, dopamine generates the desire, and it serves as motivation that leads to action. We take action because we want something; if there is no dopamine released, we won't want something, and naturally, no action will be taken.

## "Awareness" is a skill you can learn later

Of course, the children who couldn't control themselves and ended up eating the marshmallows in front of them were sure to have eaten marshmallows before. That's why, simply by looking at the marshmallows placed in front of them, they could imagine the sweetness and the gooey texture of the marshmallows and recreate the sensation of eating them. The dopamine got to work, and a desire to eat was generated that prompted them to act. It's no wonder that, faced with such temptation, they eventually became unable to control themselves.

Subjects were able to wait twice as long when they imagined that the
marshmallows were clouds.

So, in order to forgo the marshmallows, the thing to do is to not
be seduced in the first place. To do that, the children who resisted
temptation used the "cognitive" power of their cool system, which
told them how to interpret the reality in front of them.

- They were able to wait twice as long when they were
  advised to think of the marshmallows as "fluffy, circular clouds."
- They were able to wait for an average of eighteen minutes when advised to think that the marshmallows
  "weren't real."

The children were able to wait simply by changing their per-
ception of the marshmallows. The mechanism of the dopamine to

motivate them became weaker, and I'm sure that they were far less seduced than they had previously been.

The children who weren't told anything by the researchers but were able to wait anyway had good intuition to divert their attention from the marshmallows to begin with. I'm sure that they had excellent cognitive capacities in their cool system.

By offering tips on this cognitive ability, the researchers were able to help children who may have otherwise struggled put the skill into practice. What that means is that it's a skill that can be acquired.

## The cool system will also lie

Thinking of marshmallows as circular clouds or as fake is a high-level working of cognition through the cool system. In my opinion, if there's anything that can be developed, it's this cognitive capacity, and not something vague like willpower.

But there are some children who used this cool system effectively in order to "cheat." That's because the cool system is also a structure that reasons, calculates, and plans.

One child ate only the inside of a marshmallow and left the outside part to make it look like it hadn't been eaten. Another broke apart a cookie, licked the cream filling, and put it back together. These were children who ingeniously used the cool system to obtain the reward in front of them.

It's also the cool system at work when you think to yourself that although you want to lose weight and you aren't hungry, you eat "because you might get hungry later on," or come up with an excuse like "today is a day to celebrate" and indulge yourself, or tell yourself that it's okay because you "abstained yesterday and the day before that, and this is a reward."

A detailed plan to commit a crime, like in the film *Ocean's Eleven*, has to be because of the cool system, too.

Willpower isn't reliable, as it will always be affected by emotion. And the cool system can also be manipulated. It makes you wonder if we're at a dead end. What, then, should we do?

## A person with strong willpower isn't tempted in the first place

What will serve as a reference here is an experiment that was conducted in Germany that looked into the amount of temptation that people were subjected to in a day. More than two hundred subjects were made to wear beepers, which rang at random seven times a day. The subjects reported on the types of desires they felt when the beepers rang and a short while before that. The results suggest that they were fighting against some type of temptation for at least four hours every day. Fighting the desire to sleep longer, knowing that they had to get up; having to work against the desire to go out and play; fighting the temptation of a food that looked delicious. People are subjected to a similar type of desire as "I want to eat the marshmallows in front of me!" for a considerable amount of time each day.

This experiment also showed that people who were believed to have strong willpower experienced shorter periods of desire. It wasn't that they had a strong will that enabled them to repeatedly overcome temptation; they were being seduced less often to begin with.

## To worry is to call up awareness

The ability to report on a conflict that we're feeling, like the study participants did whenever their beepers rang, means we're clearly aware of a challenge and wondering what to do about it.

When I run a marathon, I can run without being aware of it when things are going well.

Marathon runner Arata Fujiwara even goes so far as to say, "I'm asleep for the first thirty kilometers." It's probably like a state of meditation.

But this won't apply if your knees start to hurt.

There will be more occasions when your conscious mind is called up: "How many more kilometers are there? Still ten more kilometers to go?" "Should I retire now?" "How many more kilometers? What? I've only run five hundred meters from that last time I thought about this?"

The reason time seems to go by more slowly when a task becomes a struggle is because you start to think about the time more often.

I'm writing this book at the library. I forget about the time when things are going well. It's what's called a state of "flow."

But when my logic doesn't connect or I get stuck in writing my manuscript, I start to think about stopping my writing. There was a time when I used an app to count the number of times that happened, and I usually left the library when it happened around ten times and I could no longer bear it.

## Decision-making is as irrational as flipping coins

There are many aspects of the human decision-making process that are extremely irrational in the first place. As an example, let's say that we'll toss a coin now. I want you to make a bet on the outcome.

You were probably able to decide right away whether you wanted to bet on heads or tails. But it's hard to explain when we're asked, "Why did you make that decision?" Although you're definitely the one who made that decision, you don't really know the reasoning behind it. When you get lost, you can tentatively choose which way to go without a particular reason.

Isn't it the same thing with the issue of whether or not to eat that marshmallow?

Mischel described seeing, over and over again in the marshmallow test, the children who couldn't control themselves suddenly reaching out to ring the bell, then looking away with anguished expressions, as if they couldn't believe what they'd done. It seems that while the actions during those times were without a doubt actions that the children had chosen to take on their own, it appeared to some degree not to have been of their own choice.

## Habits are actions that we take with barely a thought

I think that being seduced by the marshmallows is like flipping a coin. One side of the coin says: "Don't eat the marshmallow; wait," and the other, "Eat the marshmallow." We should be able to wait several times if we're lucky. But the more times we toss the coin, we'll eventually end up doing something that we don't consciously want to do.

It isn't because of weak willpower that we can't wait for our marshmallows. It's simply because we flip the coin many times. Maybe the solution, then, is to not toss the coin—or in other words, to not call up our awareness.

But our awareness is called up when there's an issue before us that we should worry about. For example, no one considers the question of whether to receive a hundred dollars or a thousand dollars an "issue" to worry about; we can make an instant decision without using our cognitive ability. It's when there are similar values in front of us, and we need to think about which is worth more, that we start to worry. Do we receive one apple today, or do we receive two apples tomorrow?

"Actions that we take with barely a thought," without calling up our awareness: I think that's what habits are. What then is this "awareness" that's called up when we worry about a lot of things?

How can people start to act well—stop themselves from eating the marshmallow—without using their awareness? How can they turn things they consciously want to do into habits? Let's take a close look at this in Chapter 2.

## Summary of Chapter 1

- Hyperbolic discounting is the human tendency to exaggerate rewards in front of us and to minimize our estimation of rewards (and punishment) in the future, making it tough to acquire good habits.

- From school performance to character, children who waited twenty minutes in order to receive an extra marshmallow in the marshmallow test demonstrated high capacities in various things once they grew up— but that doesn't necessarily mean they had a fixed, "strong willpower" from an early age.

- Willpower is not something that decreases when you simply do something.

- Willpower is affected by emotions and lost because of uncertainty and doubt. Even if you do something that requires willpower, you won't lose it, as long as you have a sense of self-esteem.

- The human brain has a cool system that's logical and a hot system that's emotional, and these systems counteract one another.

- The hot system can be controlled when we look at the things in front of us in a new way, for example, when we use the cognitive capacity in our cool system to think of marshmallows as clouds.

- Since we cannot eliminate our emotions, our willpower will always continue to be unreliable. And the cool system can always be manipulated to make deliberate lies and convenient excuses.

- People with "strong" willpower were not even aware that they were being tempted in the first place.

- The question of which reward is greater becomes an issue that we worry about if we have to call up our awareness.
- Habits are actions that we take with barely a thought. To make something a habit, it's necessary to reduce the emergence of our awareness.

CHAPTER 2

# WHAT ARE HABITS?

*There is no more miserable human being than one in whom nothing is habitual but indecision, and for whom the lighting of every cigar, the drinking of every cup, the time of rising and going to bed every day, and the beginning of every bit of work, are subjects of express volitional deliberation. Full half the time of such a man goes to the deciding, or regretting, of matters which ought to be so ingrained in him as practically not to exist for his consciousness at all.*

—William James

I wrote at the end of Chapter 1 that habits are actions that we take with barely a thought.

My belief is that when something is a habit, you're as close to acting without conscious thought as possible. In such a state, no concerns or decisions exist as to whether or not to act, and there are no choices about methods to take. This is because concerns, decisions, and choices are all issues that we handle in our conscious mind.

According to a study done at Duke University, 45 percent of our actions are habits rather than decisions made on the spot. A question comes to mind when we say that we should be thinking consciously to determine most of our actions, like whether to have curry or ramen noodles for lunch, or which movie to see on our day off. If habits are "actions we take with barely a thought," then isn't 45 percent a large percentage?

But while there may be some who can't make up their minds about which restaurant to go to for lunch, do people seriously contemplate whether or not they'll "start with a beer" when they go to a bar?

## Habits from the time we get up in the morning

Let's think about our actions after we wake up in the morning. We get up from bed, go to the bathroom, and take a shower. We eat breakfast, brush our teeth, get dressed, tie our shoelaces, and leave the house.

Everyone has a unique set of procedures, and isn't our morning flow like a ritual from the moment that we get up?

We don't usually think about how much toothpaste to use when we brush our teeth or which tooth to start with, and we don't think about how we're going to tie our shoelaces that day. Since we can do these things without thinking, there should be few people who consider their morning ritual difficult or an effort. We can say that these things are habits for most adults.

But for small children, this series of actions in the morning takes a lot of effort. They can't go to the bathroom by themselves, there are obstacles to brushing their teeth, buttoning their clothes, and tying their shoelaces, and it takes tremendous patience to overcome them. They might exhaust their willpower even before leaving their homes, and sulk in bed. But they'll be able to do these things automatically after continued repetitions. These are mostly subconscious movements for adults, and we can't understand why it's difficult for children to do them.

## Can you explain every tap you make on your smartphone?

Of course, there are things we have to learn after we grow up. Last year, I started driving a car again for the first time in eighteen years, after obtaining my license. At first, I was going through each procedure in my head—fasten the seat belt, step on the brakes, turn the key, release the hand brake, shift the gear from "park" to "drive." I'm now driving a more complicated manual-transmission car, but my hands and feet move without the need to think about anything, and it's tough to explain each procedure in this way.

Before I became used to driving, there was a need to focus my awareness, and I felt like I was looking at an incredible god when I saw anyone driving while they listened to music. But I can now drive without thinking about it while directing my attention chiefly to my English audio study material.

It's probably the same with people who ride a bicycle. Even if they don't drive a car, perhaps it's difficult for them to explain the procedure of how to pedal a bike, or offer tips on maintaining your balance. I wonder if people who are always tapping on their smartphones are able to explain, without using their hands, how they're entering each vowel or consonant.

## People who cook or drive while sleepwalking

As a child I was terrified of cracking eggs—I was always nervous, like I was handling something incredibly precious. I think I had my awareness working to a considerable degree the first time that

I cooked eggs sunny-side up. How much oil to use, how strong the heat should be. Now I no longer have to do a recipe search for eggs sunny-side up, or for hard-boiled eggs; my hands move automatically.

My mother knows how to cook an array of dishes, and even if we're in the middle of dinner, if the neighbors bring something over, she can cook it right away. She doesn't need to check recipes on cooking sites, and she doesn't need to measure the seasonings. She says she can come up with ideas about what to cook when she looks at ingredients. She also says she's never thought it "troublesome" to cook. Those of us who don't often cook think it's "troublesome" because we're pondering the procedures, which is proof that our awareness is at work. My mother can cook without giving it a second thought; that's probably why she doesn't think it's troublesome.

Sleepwalking patients sometimes cook or drive during deep non-REM sleep, and they don't remember these actions later on. While the part of the brain that monitors these movements is asleep, the part that directs complicated actions is working. In other words, people can act in complicated ways, even if they aren't "aware."

I don't think ants are supposed to have a cognitive awareness, either, but they dig holes, carry sand, and always work hard. Ants don't need business books. They can work without relying on things like motivation or enthusiasm.

## Awareness is like a newspaper

It's possible to take complicated actions without cognitive awareness. On the other hand, this awareness is what we usually think of as making us "ourselves." It lets us perceive the beautiful scenery in front of us, and it causes us to care about the things that people say to us.

What in the world is this cognitive awareness that people have?

In his book, *Incognito: The Secret Lives of the Brain*, neuroscientist David Eagleman says the conscious mind is like a newspaper.

This is what happens every day in a given country: Factories are in operation and companies deliver their products. The police track criminals, doctors conduct operations, and lovers go on dates. Electricity flows through power lines, and waste is passed through sewers. But people have neither the ability nor the desire to know about all events that are going on in their country. That's why there's a need to summarize only the important things, and that's why we have newspapers.

In a newspaper headline, we don't expect to find out the amount of grass that such-and-such a number of cows in the country ate yesterday, or how many thousands of cows were shipped; we only want to be warned if there's a sudden rise in the incidence of mad cow disease. We don't want to know how many tons of garbage were disposed of yesterday; we only want to know if a new waste processing plant will be set up in our neighborhood.

In the same way, it isn't as if our conscious mind wants to process all the details of what's happening in the sixty trillion cells in our

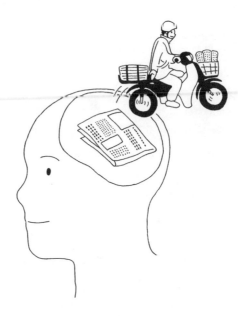

Awareness is like a newspaper.

bodies, or the interactions of electric signals in the thousands of neurons within us. While the brain processes 11 million bits of information every second, it's estimated that only 50 bits of information are processed in our conscious mind. Like a newspaper reporter, the neural circuit in our brain gathers massive amounts of data behind the scenes in our subconscious mind. And as with a newspaper, only the summaries are delivered to our conscious mind.

## Which shoe did you put on first this morning, the right or the left?

Your awareness is not called up when you're repeating the same actions as always, without any problems—just as no articles are produced about an ordinary subject if there are no incidents. The reason why it's tough to correct habits like crossing your legs or slouching is because they occur without your awareness.

Few people clearly remember which shoe they put on first this morning, their right or their left. It's because the question of which shoe to put on first isn't determined by your conscious mind; it's generally already decided.

Neuroscientist Yuji Ikegaya offers an interesting example. "We can always see our nose, but we aren't conscious of it." True, our nose is always in our field of vision, and we can see it if we desire. But it isn't the type of news that has to be printed in a newspaper.

## Times when our conscious mind is called up

Let's imagine a situation where our conscious mind is called up. Think about when you walk. We have more than two hundred bones in our bodies, more than a hundred joints, and four hundred skeletal muscles, and each of these parts works in close coordination with the others. The reason why it's tough to make a robot walk is because you need to program and teach it everything, from how to move and angle each individual part, to how to use feedback from the soles of the feet to determine and adjust to the surface of the floor.

We don't need to have a conscious thought about walking; we can stroll at our leisure.

But even then, our awareness will be called up if we step on something tender.

*Squish.* "What was that? Dang!"

## The newspaper when you have a stomachache

I'm sure that everyone has experienced getting a stomachache at school. Even if it happens during a class in which you're usually happy to kill time spacing out, dozing off, or doodling, the situation will suddenly change. A newspaper headline will be delivered to your conscious mind:

> "Abnormality in the stomach. Possibility of a stomachache."

> "Determined as a stomachache. Is it because I ate too much at lunch?"

> "Thirty minutes remaining in class. What will happen to the stomachache issue?"

> "Respite in stomachache, leading to moments of peace."

A lot of newspapers get delivered—our conscious mind is called up frequently—which means we can't concentrate, and the usual duration of time seems terribly long. Just as newspaper headlines are only made when incidents occur, our awareness is only called up when something different happens.

## Do people have free will?

*While they may be aware of their actions, they are ignorant*
*of the causes by which they are determined.*
—Baruch Spinoza

Surely awareness is what leads our mind. It considers things and determines our actions. But most day-to-day actions are taken not according to directions given by our leaders, but instead by the townspeople, on their own initiative.

You're doing something and feel tired. You stretch without being aware of it; you don't think, "Okay, I'll raise the palms of the hands I've clasped together and stretch." It isn't the leader who decided that you would stretch.

A famous experiment conducted during the 1980s by physiologist Benjamin Libet shows how unreliable this leader, awareness, can be. The people who participated moved their fingers (or their wrists) whenever they wanted, and records were taken of their brain activity, to determine:

1. The moment that each subject made the decision to move the fingers
2. The moment that a command signal for motion occurred in the brain
3. The moment that the fingers actually moved

The results? Surprisingly, the sequence of events turned out to be 2 > 1 > 3. The command signal for motion occurred an average of 0.35 seconds before the subjects thought they'd made their decision. The brain started to prepare to move the fingers before the subjects decided to do so.

This experiment gathered a lot of attention; it had the potential to refute the idea of free will. But actions can never be incurred from nothing, and there must be some type of brain activity that occurs before the action.

## Who's the DJ that chooses which tunes to hum?

What about humming? Humming is different from making a selection on a jukebox or at a karaoke bar. With a jukebox, you make a conscious choice about what song you'd like to listen to or sing along to. But I doubt that anyone thinks, "Which song shall I sing?" before they hum a tune that comes to mind naturally.

Sometimes the songs I hum are simply those that happened to be playing at the supermarket that I just went to; I'm not in the least bit interested in singing them. These are songs that the DJ in a place beyond my awareness has gone ahead and chosen.

Consider our intestines. There are more than a hundred million nerve cells in a person's intestines, which are connected to the brain through the vagus nerve. But even if the vagus nerve were to be cut off, the intestines would still make independent decisions. Thus, the gut is sometimes called "the second brain." But can you imagine your stomach being your second in command?

## Our actions are determined by something like a parliamentary system

> *It has been said that democracy is the worst form of govern-*
> *ment except for all those other forms that have been tried.*
> —Winston Churchill

Unconscious actions are determined on a case-by-case basis, but not by an absolute monarchy. We might think of it as a parliamentary system.

Let's take getting up in the morning as an example. The alarm clock rings at the time you decided on beforehand, when you said you would "get up at such-and-such time, starting tomorrow." But when the alarm actually goes off, it's not the end of the matter; instead, it's a signal that parliament is about to convene.

Politicians assemble from various parts of your body, and the session gets under way. Your lower back has awakened, and you have a little pain there. Because of that, the politician elected from the lower back region grumpily says, "We should still be asleep." You also ate too much at an event last might. The politician that from the gut region says, "Let us slowly digest."

It's time to vote, and the majority vote is to "get some more sleep." You hit the snooze button—a decision has been made to sleep for five more minutes. More votes take place every five minutes, until the parts of you that want to eat a nice breakfast or want to get to work on time gradually become more persuasive. And finally, despite all the fuss, you get out of bed.

## When an unconscious action has become a habit

Once getting up early has become a habit, the motion to "get up right away" is passed in a short period with majority vote, despite a little opposition.

It's important to understand that parliament will still be held, even if you did everything right to prepare to make a good decision, and opposing opinions won't stop being presented completely. I make sure to get plenty of sleep, but of course, there are times when I can get up feeling clear and refreshed and times when I don't feel like that at all.

When I don't want to get up, I always think the same thing: "Maybe I've accumulated fatigue." I have this thought constantly, and I sometimes wonder if I can trust the idea that it's time to start my day, even if that thought is also coming from me.

But if I haven't been able to make it a habit to get up early, I know I won't be able to stick to any of my other habits, either, and I know that I'll feel down. And I also remind myself that as long as I get up and do some yoga, I'll be wide awake in five minutes, even if I'm a little tired right when the alarm goes off. Because I've repeated this inner debate over and over, the result has basically become fixed. So, my inner parliamentary system doesn't have to keep repeating the voting.

## We are not our kings

As we've seen so far, many actions that people take are not driven by their awareness. But it's our awareness that feels responsible when we don't do what we're supposed to do. It's easy to conclude that it's because of a person's "weak will," and an issue of their awareness, if they don't succeed at dieting or quitting cigarettes or alcohol.

But that's a show of overconfidence in our awareness and will-power, based on the misunderstanding that a person's awareness significantly controls their actions.

What we must first keep in mind is that awareness and will-power are not the causes behind our actions. Unfortunately, we are not our kings. We must calmly acknowledge that fact.

## Making yourself a creature of habit

In the autumn, squirrels try to secure plenty of food in prepara-tion for winter. But it isn't as if squirrels think consciously, "The winter's about to come, so I'd better secure lots of food," or make a detailed plan. The brains of squirrels have evolved so that when the sunlight that enters their vision decreases a certain amount, a pro-gram is activated that instructs them to start burying their food.

Haruki Murakami has said that his life philosophy is to make himself a "creature of habit." To form a habit is to change the part of yourself that's an animal—the part that's governed by your unconscious. The issue isn't something in your conscious mind, it's the amount of sunlight that enters your vision. To change your habits, you need to better address the real source that governs your actions.

Let's take a look at how our actions become habits. It's the process by which the king that we call our awareness steps down from the position of king.

## Forming habits without thinking

To learn to ride a bicycle without thinking, we need to learn how to use our bodies. At first, we need to control our movements using our awareness, but eventually we ride without thinking about it. What types of changes occur in our brain when that happens?

An experiment conducted at MIT during the 1990s can serve as a reference. Devices were embedded in the heads of rats to study their brain activity. The rats were placed at the entrance of a T-shaped maze, with chocolate placed around the left bend. The partitions were removed when a clicking sound was made as a cue, at which time the rats would try to find the source of the sweet smell. It took time, at first, as they went back and forth and kept turning in the opposite direction.

As the trial and error continued, activity took place in the part of the rat's brain called the basal ganglia.

After the experiment was repeated hundreds of times, the rats stopped losing their way, and it took less time for them to reach their goal. The rats became very good at finding the chocolate, but their brain activity actually decreased; they "thought" less and less.

Two or three days after the experiment began, they would scratch the walls, sniff the scent, and could then stop gathering

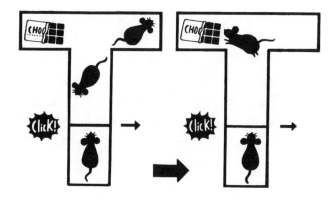

To find the chocolate, a rat first goes through trial and error. But after many
repetitions, the rat's brain activity decreases; it stops having to "think."

information; they knew enough already. And by the time a week
had gone by, activity had also decreased in the part of their brain
associated with memory. In the end, the rats were able to get to the
chocolate without thinking at all. The action had become a habit.

## The three elements of habits

According to Charles Duhigg, author of *The Power of Habit*, habits consist of the following three elements:

*Trigger.* The rats' brains were most active when they heard the
sound of the partitions being removed and when they eventually
found the chocolate. The trigger conveys what "autopilot mode" to
use—in the rats' case, the clicking sound.

*Routine.* A trigger leads to a predetermined set of actions, a routine. In the case of the rats, the routine became to turn left at the

bend, without hesitation, as soon as the maze was opened, thus finding the chocolate. This routine was put together as a result of trial and error and stored in the rats' brains, and became a series of actions that could eventually be taken with barely a thought.

*Reward.* The brain determines whether a series of actions should be stored as a routine based on the reward. As we saw in Chapter 1, a reward is something that brings us joy and happiness; it's something that feels good. For the rats, it's smart to take the same actions that result in finding tasty chocolate. That's why their brains worked on storing the path to that chocolate.

## Making something a habit is to cause an actual change in your brain

We go back to a restaurant where the food was good, and we don't go again if it tasted bad. We repeatedly try to experience emotions like happiness and joy that we feel as a result of our actions. This "reward system," which is activated through the mediation of dopamine, is an old circuit, and it works the same way in rats and humans. And when we take actions like eating, having sex, or interacting with friends, we experience pleasant feelings.

And the more we conduct these actions, the stronger the link between the actions and the pleasant feelings becomes. A dendritic spine, which is a membranous protrusion that receives signals at the synapse and allows nerve cells to pass signals between them, will actually become bigger when it repeatedly receives signals.

Making something a habit is completely different from learning something using your awareness, like if you listen to a lecture or take part in a seminar. It means practicing something over and over to actually rewrite the nerve cells in the brain.

## My triggers: yoga and my diary

Let's take a more detailed look at each element of a habit.

First, we have the trigger. The general concept should be familiar to everyone—for example, it's common to use an alarm clock as a trigger to get up in the morning. What I do next is yoga. I lay out my yoga mat on the floor before going to bed, so it's the first thing that I see in the morning. That becomes a trigger, and I'm spurred to do yoga right after I get up.

I also make coffee in the morning, after eating breakfast. Drinking that coffee is my trigger to start writing in my diary. When I drank coffee one evening, I wanted to write in my diary, because coffee is connected with my morning routine of writing in my diary.

A story in *The Principles of Psychology* by William James goes like this: A war veteran carries his meal in both arms. Another man jokingly says, "Attention!" and the veteran reacts to the trigger and lowers both his arms to stand "at attention," dropping the meat and potatoes he had been carrying. Habit functioned more powerfully than his awareness of the important things he was holding.

## Small triggers that create gifted people

There are times when a small trigger serves as the beginning for creating a genius. Mayu Yamaguchi graduated from the Faculty of Law at University of Tokyo at the top of her class, served as an official at the Ministry of Finance, and then became a lawyer, completing law school at Harvard University with straight As. She obtained qualification as a lawyer from the State of New York, and says she is now aiming to become a university professor of law.

No matter how I look at it, I can only imagine from this tremendous personal history, which almost gives me heartburn, that she has to be a genius. But Yamaguchi says what other geniuses say: "I'm not a genius, so I had to make an effort." Her studies began by looking at her desk.

This is the habit Yamaguchi has maintained since childhood. She gets up in the morning, opens the drapes, and lets in the sunlight. Next, she turns her eyes to her desk. She would sit at her desk and read a book—any book would do—for around ten minutes, until her mother would call out to her to say that breakfast was ready. Yamaguchi says this routine has always helped remove any sense of resistance she may have had to sitting at her desk during the day. She would later come home from school, have a snack, and begin studying again, starting over with the familiar step of taking a seat at her desk.

During high school and law school, each morning she would bathe in the morning light and then look at her desk before getting to work. This habit, which began from such a small trigger, created a genius.

## Triggers for habits that you want to quit

Unfortunately, habits that you want to quit function the exact same way. I wanted to cut down on my drinking, but it was difficult.

One reason was that there were many "buddies" for alcohol that served as triggers. For example, I liked to start drinking beer in the afternoon, and I would reflexively order bottled beer if I ordered soba noodles with tempura. The same applied to greasy foods like *gyoza* and fried chicken. Many other items also brought along the beer.

Charles Duhigg summarizes five types of triggers as follows. I'll give examples of triggers that make us want to drink.

- Location (a convenience store on your way home; the venue for a friend's wedding)
- Time (when you finish work in the evening; Sunday afternoons)
- Emotional state (stress from continuously working overtime; feeling down after making a mistake)
- Other people (a date with a lovely lady; a class reunion with people you haven't seen in a while)
- Preceding event (working up a sweat while exercising; taking a dip in a hot spring spa)

We'll look at these in detail in Chapter 3, but first, it's important to identify the triggers for a habit you want to quit, and to establish new triggers for a habit that you want to acquire.

## Routines that connect like a chain

> *I don't do special things for the purpose of doing something special. I do ordinary, everyday things in order to do something special.*
>
> —Ichiro

"Routines" are easy to understand. They refer to a set of actions that begin with a trigger. Brushing your teeth when you start getting ready for bed, using a hair dryer after taking a shower; these are actions that abound in our everyday life.

When I go to the gym, my initial trigger is the itch to move my body. And as usual, I prepare my gym clothes and my water bottle. The path to the gym and the method for unlocking my locker are ingrained. My program is set for my muscle training and running, and the same goes for taking a shower after exercising and the method for washing my gym clothes.

One routine serves as a trigger for starting the next routine. Although going to the gym to exercise is a complicated action, it's possible to consider it as a series of actions where the triggers and the routine are connected like a chain. The same goes for everyone's morning rituals.

## Routines give the mind a tune-up

The good thing about routines is that you can change your mood simply by doing what you always do. Routines function like a tuner.

For example, Haruki Murakami says that although he runs for

an hour each day, he runs for a little bit longer when he receives unwarranted criticism or a rejection from someone. I, too, run every day, even more so when something negative happens. It's because I have a real sense that my mood changes when I do that. The essence of the problem isn't in the problem itself; it's an issue of my mood, meaning, how to view the problem. We've seen that emotions affect willpower. By practicing your regular routine, the negative emotions will be eliminated, and your willpower will recover.

As to how he overcomes tough times, Ichiro says he "does what he does every day, the same way as always." He explains, "It's difficult to start with the mind, but it will eventually catch up when I move the way that I always do. It's a technique for times when my mind isn't proactive."

You can tune up your mind by using your body as you always do. Your breathing gets faster when you feel that you "want" something, like when you're about to buy something on impulse. So, the desire gets settled down when you intentionally breathe slowly. You can do this to calm yourself more easily when you've made it a habit to meditate.

Rugby player Goromaru makes a sign with his fingers before he kicks the ball, and Yuzuru Hanyu makes the sign of the cross before he skates. They probably have to regain balance when they become enthusiastic or jittery for their own reasons, like, "This will be the deciding kick."

Going through the same routine to get back to your usual, relaxed psychological state, and producing the results that you've been practicing for. This is why athletes rely on routines.

## Rewards that are tough for people to imagine

> *"That's . . . a narcotic."*
> *" . . . A narcotic?"*
> *"Yes. Once you plaster yourself to a rock wall on a mountain and inhale it, your everyday life will seem lukewarm."*
> —*The Summit of the Gods*

The third element of habits, reward, is surprisingly the most difficult to fully understand. People attempt an action over and over to seek a reward:

- Eating something good
- Interacting with friends
- Having sex with someone you love
- Earning money
- Getting likes on social media

These are rewards that are easy to understand, and actions to pursue them are also easy to understand. But there are some actions that make you wonder why a person would do something like that.

## The reward for writing on Wikipedia

When we talk about rewards, we can't help thinking about money, but that's not all there is. For example, you won't receive a single dollar for writing a Wikipedia article.

I was told that a writer by the name of Norimaki spent six

months writing an article about Kobayashi Issa. That's a tremendous amount of work. Norimaki says Wikipedia is a place where you can greedily research something that intrigues you and explore and share that interest as much as you like.

You can satisfy your curiosity and inquisitiveness, and present it at a venue that other people will see. That must be the type of reward that motivates the writers on Wikipedia. Similarly, other kinds of writers will share their work with one another, and "meetups" are held for people who have the same hobbies. Finding such a community of matching interests is also a kind of reward.

Microsoft once hired an expensive manager, gathered professional writers, and attempted to create a dictionary. Money was the reward. But it was nowhere near as powerful as the energy that people are able to produce when they act on their own accord. Even if there's no money involved, people can experience various types of "rewards."

## What type of reward do you get for tough exercise?

Many forms of reward are difficult for others to imagine. I used to see people running under the blazing summer sun and think, "What's in it for them, doing something like that?"

Even though I belonged to the basketball club in junior high, where I worked hard and never missed a single day of practice, I stopped exercising once I grew up. I would think to myself, "I don't know what's so fun about running."

I'm now running full marathons again, and people sometimes say to me, "I just can't understand why you do something like that." For those who are not in the habit of running, thinking about it just brings images of suffering. But if rewards are necessary for habits, then there must be some reward in the pain of running as well.

## Does running really release endorphins?

The neurotransmitters called endorphins are often used to explain the rewards of running. Endorphins have an analgesic effect, like morphine, so they control the pain of running and bring on a euphoric experience—what's called a "runner's high."

The neuroscientist Gregory Berns questions that explanation, however. In one study, true beta-endorphins only increased in 50 percent of people engaged in strenuous exercise. Even among runners, there are few who have actually experienced "runner's high," and even they don't experience it every time they run. Berns believes that endorphins don't cause euphoria, but are some type of by-product.

## The positive functions of stress hormones

Then what is the reward of running? Berns believes the answer lies in the stress hormone cortisol. You would think that stress hormones are just the bad guys—but just as dopamine has a complicated function, cortisol is versatile.

Here's how Berns explains it: Cortisol is generated in particularly high amounts by physical stress, and it lifts your mood, boosts your concentration, and may, depending on the situation, enhance your memory. But these effects are only present with twenty to forty milligrams amount of secretion in a day; any more than that will cause uncertainty or symptoms of what we'd call stress.

Just the right amount of cortisol will interact with dopamine and cause a strong sense of satisfaction, or even a transcendental level of euphoria. Berns actually had the appropriate amount of cortisol administered to his own body, and reported euphoria and happiness. He concluded that dopamine alone isn't enough. Combining it with the cortisol that's excreted with a moderate level of stress will allow you to obtain a powerful sense of satisfaction.

For me, too, around ten minutes after I start running, I start to feel different; just moving my body starts to become a joy in itself. It should be more convenient for living organisms to conserve calories in order to survive, and we humans probably want to take it easy. But at a certain point after I've started to run, I have a sense that I've switched to a different mode.

My worries and concerns become distant, I start to feel energized, and I'm more full of enthusiasm and confidence than I am in my everyday life. It's tough, of course, to be in a state where I'm out of breath, but appropriate physical stress prolongs my sense of satisfaction for a while after I've finished running.

We wouldn't have to go to the trouble of physical exertion, like running, if we only needed to release dopamine to experience euphoria. That's because there are plenty of other ways to release dopamine, like eating tasty foods. But when we're talking about a truly powerful sense of satisfaction, what's necessary is an appropriate amount of pain, not to mention stress.

## The reasons why Bill Gates and Jeff Bezos work

Bill Gates and Jeff Bezos shouldn't have to work—they have enough wealth to lie on the beach at a resort until they die, and yet they don't choose to do that. Perhaps it's because they can't feel a powerful sense of satisfaction if they're only doing fun things.

I was once jilted by a girlfriend who said, "Hey, we only seem to be doing things that are fun!" I thought I had been coming up with great date ideas so that she could enjoy herself when she was with me. So, when she said that to me, I thought, "Huh? I don't know what you're talking about!" But I think I can now see what she meant.

Our sense of satisfaction also probably becomes stronger in interpersonal relationships where we have stress. Dramas are interesting because they have ups and downs and climaxes. The script that I'd written was a bad one, where only fun things happened.

I've gotten sidetracked; there are more rewards to exercising. For example, everyone must have the experience of coming up with an idea not while sitting at their desk and thinking, but while taking a walk or exercising.

Mason Currey's *Daily Rituals: How Artists Work* is an introduction to the daily habits of creative people like authors and musicians, and a lot of them—you can almost say most of them—have a daily routine of taking walks.

In writing this very book, a lot of my ideas came to mind while I was running. Exercise enables us to tap into a type of creativity that's different from what we experience when we're sitting at a desk.

## Aerobic exercises develop your neurons

In *Spark: The Revolutionary New Science of Exercise and the Brain*, John Ratey says frankly that exercise makes us feel refreshed because when we get our blood pumping, it makes the brain function at its best.

This is the rationale Ratey, a professor of psychiatry at Harvard Medical School, gives for the exercises he describes as beneficial for the brain. Besides neurotransmitters, there's a protein group in the brain called a factor. And this brain-derived neurotrophic factor (BDNF) increases with aerobic exercise. When BDNF is sprinkled on neurons, they sprout new branches; neurons are like trees that have these synapses at the ends of the branches in place of leaves. The synapses increase when new branches are formed, making the connections between them even stronger.

Ratey says BDNF is like fertilizer for the brain.

## A school where performance improved with exercise

One traditional strategy to improve your grades is to increase the amount of study time with books and textbooks. But it isn't that simple in real life—and sometimes physical exercise can help, instead.

In 2003, a high school in Naperville, Illinois, launched an initiative called "Zero Hour PE" for nineteen thousand students, who ran on the field or exercised on stationary bikes before their first class.

The results were tremendous. While students who only took regular PE classes improved by 10.7 percent in their reading and comprehension tests, those who took "Zero Hour PE" showed an improvement of 17 percent. The students in Naperville took global standard mathematics and science tests called TIMSS (Trends in International Mathematics and Science Study), and ranked sixth in the world in math and first in the world in science (the average performance by American students was eighteenth in science and nineteenth in mathematics). Exercising before commencing their schoolwork enhanced the effects of their studying, and their performance improved.

In a 2007 study conducted by a German group of researchers, subjects were able to learn vocabulary 20 percent faster after, rather than before, they exercised, revealing the correlation between learning efficiency and BDNF values.

Rewards are necessary for habits. People who exercise a lot are often thought of as highly self-disciplined. But it isn't as though people like that abstain from receiving rewards. They just receive rewards that are much greater than monetary compensation.

## Habits are just like other addictions

But no matter how much I write about it, I think it's probably hard for people who aren't in the habit of exercising to imagine what makes it worth the effort.

A reward that you can understand only after acquiring a habit is like a beer for someone who's never had it before. The refreshing taste of a cold beer on a hot day, and the good feeling of being tipsy, can't be conveyed with words, no matter how you try to explain it.

I've never played a slot machine, so I don't understand the gambler's euphoria from getting a hit. For someone who doesn't smoke, it's hard to imagine what's fun about paying a lot of money to inhale and exhale smoke that gives you a headache. Beer, gambling, cigarettes—even if you partake in all these things, you probably don't have a good understanding of why a cocaine addict gets excited when they see white powder.

Actions like exercise that may appear ascetic and actions like seeking drugs aren't actually much different in terms of structure. People will repeat the same actions in pursuit of rewards. That essential element will not falter, and I think the process works like an addiction.

People find it hard to imagine that others have different types of rewards from those that they receive themselves. That's why people who run appear, to people who don't run, to be losing out.

Acquiring a habit is just like learning to like beer: it's only bitter at the beginning. You endure that bitterness at first and keep trying it repeatedly, until one day, it becomes your favorite drink.

Acquiring a habit isn't about bolstering your willpower so that you can overcome temptation. It's rewriting the "rewards" and "punishments." It's causing a change in your brain, by taking action over and over again.

## Tips for habits: How to divert your eyes from the marshmallows

In Chapter 1, I offered an introduction to the marshmallow test. What would happen if instead of taking the test just once, subjects were to take it repeatedly?

The first time around, a reward of two marshmallows in twenty minutes is too abstract to really wrap your head around. And resisting the marshmallow in front of you during that time is painful if you aren't experienced.

But by succeeding a number of times, you would acquire the skill to think about fun things to divert your attention from the marshmallow, or to imagine that it's not real. And if you get two marshmallows after waiting for twenty minutes a repeated number of times, you'll start to gain a real sense of the reward.

Among the children who successfully obtained the two marshmallows were some who didn't eat them right away. They wanted to take the two marshmallows home and receive praise from their mothers for the great feat that they had accomplished. The children wanted a reward that was greater than eating two marshmallows right away.

This is what it means to acquire a good habit. It is not as if the alluring things in front of you disappear. But when you keep obtaining big rewards in the future, the reward in front of you will start to look boring.

It's true that willpower is needed when you try to acquire a new habit. It isn't easy, and there's no magic way to do it. But once you do, you're able to continue the habit, because there's a big reward that surely awaits you.

In the next chapter, I divide up the method for making something into a habit into fifty steps, and go over each of them in detail.

You can't overcome the marshmallows in front of you without a strategy. The trick to acquiring a habit is to divert your eyes from the marshmallows through every possible means, until you can gain a sense of the big reward.

## Summary of Chapter 2

- 45 percent of people's actions are habits.
- Actions like brushing your teeth, buttoning your shirt, and tying your shoelaces, which were difficult when you were a child, become things that you can do unconsciously as you repeat them.
- Complicated actions like driving a car or cooking can also become automatic.
- Our conscious mind is only called up when a problem occurs, and our actions and lives usually go on as if on autopilot.
- Even when an issue arises that you should worry about, like having to get up at a certain time in the morning, your conscious mind doesn't make a decision for you to follow—instead, a discussion is held in your unconscious mind, like at parliament. Rejections and approvals will occur, depending on the situation, and

you can't tell while your awareness is being called up which way a decision will be made.

- As shown in an experiment using rats, the brain gradually stops thinking when the same actions are taken repeatedly in pursuit of a reward.

- Habits are *routines* that are activated by *triggers*, and they take place as you seek *rewards*.

- Making something into a habit means you're rewriting a reward. While there are big rewards, like a sense of satisfaction or even euphoria for an act like strenuous exercise, you can't gain a sense of that big reward unless you experience it several times.

- Making something into a habit is like taking the marshmallow test over and over again. If you've obtained two marshmallows on several occasions, you'll start to feel strongly that the future reward is so great that the easier option, the reward in the present, isn't worth considering.

- The way to make something a habit is to use all means to continue to divert your eyes from the marshmallow in front of you.

CHAPTER 3

# 50 STEPS FOR
# ACQUIRING NEW HABITS

# Step 1: Sever ties with vicious circles

*To dye a dirty cloth, you must first wash it.*
—A teaching of Ayurveda

As we saw in Chapter 1, your willpower will be lost if you give in to negative emotions like uncertainty or doubt. When that happens, the brain takes instinctive action, and tells you to try to grab the reward in front of you. As a result, you may eat or drink too much, or lose the motivation to do anything and end up playing with your smartphone. Then, later, you regret those actions, and feel more stress.

To make things worse, when you're exposed to that type of stress over extended periods, the cognitive functions of your cooling system—which should control instinctive actions—will deteriorate. What you don't use will deteriorate. And a deterioration in your cognitive function means you'll no longer be able to see reality from a different perspective—for example, you won't be able to imagine that the marshmallow in front of you isn't real, or think of it as just a cloud. So you become further inclined to grab the reward in front of you.

Before long, you'll start suffering from "learned helplessness." A dog that continues to be struck by an unavoidable electric shock will continue to accept it, even after it becomes possible to jump and avoid the shock. This is because the dog tells itself that trying to avoid the shock is useless, whatever it does.

Unfortunately, there are such frameworks of vicious circles for humans, too. To acquire good habits, it's necessary to cut ties with them.

## GOOD HABIT INHIBITOR:
## Believing that a bad habit is necessary to relieve stress

It is often easy to convince yourself that some poor habits, like eating or drinking excessively, are necessary for relieving stress. Remember, you're more likely to choose the reward in front of you if you're feeling down or stressed. Stress from work or family life is inevitable; the key thing is to differentiate between the stress itself, and the additional stress that you feel from the actions that you take to resolve that stress.

There's a quote from *The Little Prince* that goes something like this: "I drink to forget that I am ashamed of drinking." Similarly, when people feel a sense of uncertainty about their finances, they will often run off shopping in a bid to escape from that uncertainty. When they are uncertain, they take an action that creates more uncertainty. But, as the author Gretchen Rubin says, we can't do something that will make us feel worse simply to cope.

## The tips for making or kicking habits
## are complete opposites

Whether habits are good or bad, they are made up of the same structures. So, to kick a habit that you now have, you can do the exact opposite of these tips for acquiring habits. For example, Step 13 is to lower the hurdle, in which case a tip for quitting a habit would be to raise the hurdle. I will follow this up with some points to consider when deciding whether you want to quit a habit. Then I'll explain the tips for quitting bad habits, along with the tips for acquiring good habits.

# Step 2: First, decide that you're going to quit

*It is well to yield up pleasure, if pain will also leave with it.*
—Publius Syrus

Everyone finds a way to fill their day somehow, whether with a busy schedule, or a lot of time spent slacking off. Whether good or bad, a day in the life of any given person is filled with habits.

So, if you want to add new habits, your old habits must make an exit. The first thing to do is decide to quit. But *which* habits should you quit? It's a difficult question; like I said, it's easy to believe something is necessary to relieve stress.

## Do you want your child to have that habit?

A question that's worth asking yourself on such an occasion is whether it's a habit that you would like your kid to have. This question works even if you don't actually have a child.

Something that's become indispensable for you, but that you would actually want to quit if you could; something that teaches you so little that you couldn't agree to your child starting to do it, too; something that leaves you with a sense of regret, rather than a sense of achievement or satisfaction.

We can come up with various excuses for not being able to quit these kinds of habits. It's also possible to concoct any number of advantages to keeping them.

But it's different when we consider whether we would like our children to have that something as a habit. I don't think there are many people who would like their children to become addicted to alcohol or nicotine, glued to their smartphone or social media, or absorbed in gambling.

It's strange that we find ourselves allowed to act as we wish when we grow up. If you think there's a need to set an hour as a time limit for your children to watch TV or play video games, then that's also necessary for an adult. We all need to continue learning until the moment that we die.

## The problem isn't the category itself

The problem is that that "something" that we should quit doing can't be dismissed simply because of its category. For example, the only memories that I have of my childhood are of playing video games, which I stopped doing when I was around thirty. I certainly must have enjoyed playing video games, yet I think once I quit, I began to look coldly at people who were absorbed in gaming.

But I changed my way of thinking when I discovered how professional gamer Daigo Umehara approaches gaming.

He, too, says that he's long been bored of the games themselves. But when winning at a gaming competition is treated as a method, the ultimate objective becomes a kind of personal growth. To gain top ranking in the world, you have to play video games seriously for hours, take notes on the issues you encounter, and make repeated improvements. The process of trial and error is no different than that undertaken by an athlete.

In short, what this means is that there is value to anything if you take it seriously. If you're able to feel that you have learned all about life from video games, then there's no need to stop playing them. I quit drinking alcohol, but I respect sommeliers and master brewers of sake who take their work seriously. There are probably people who have learned everything from liquor.

But when I look back and think about my own experience with liquor, I can't say that I gained great joy from it. Opportunities to drink are certainly fun, but there were often times that I felt regret the next day. So, I quit cold turkey.

- The things that you don't want your children to acquire
- Things that do not leave you with a sense that you have learned a lot when you reflect on it later on
- The things that leave you with regret rather than a sense of achievement

Keep these things in mind, and think about what you should quit doing.

## All actions are addictive

Stimulation in reasonable doses is necessary in life. The problem is when you want to quit but you can't. Things that you can't quit on your own are addictions. It isn't just alcohol and nicotine—there are many substances that are addictive. Sugar is one example.

In an experiment conducted by neuroscientist Nicole Avena, rats were given sugar. Over time, the rats began to show a strong desire for the sugar, built up a level of tolerance for it, as we see with drugs like cocaine, and even experienced withdrawal symptoms. When researchers at the University of Michigan conducted a survey of 384 adults, 92 percent responded that they had strong urges for certain foods, and that they failed to stop eating them despite numerous attempts.

It isn't just substances that are addictive. According to Jon Grant at University of Chicago Medicine, all things that give us an excessive reward—like excessive happiness (euphoria) or comfort—are addictive. Not just taking drugs, but eating particular foods, shopping, having sex, shoplifting, using social media—all these actions have an addictive nature. Put simply, the reason why I run is that it feels good, and you could say that I'm addicted to it.

## You often become susceptible to addictions if the rewards come quickly

A characteristic of things that are easily addictive is that the rewards come quickly. In other words, a good feeling has immediate effects. If the euphoria that you get from liquor came six hours after drinking, fewer people would enjoy it. There wouldn't be so many people hooked on social media if the "likes" arrived in your mailbox a month later.

It isn't possible for your brain to differentiate whether "good dopamine" was incurred by exercise or "bad dopamine" was increased through drugs. Your brain only tells you to repeat the actions that resulted in the pleasure. So, it is necessary to explicitly consider what it is that we should quit doing.

## The reason I quit drinking

The first habit that I wanted to quit was liquor. Mind you, I am in no way rejecting the culture associated with liquor, and I don't believe that everyone should quit drinking right now. I would never think of something like that, even if my life depended on it. It's just that for me, drinking had become something that I should stop doing.

I'll continue to talk about quitting drinking as an example, and I hope that while reading, you will replace that with whatever it is you would like to quit doing, because the strategy for quitting something is generally the same.

Now, the tough thing about drinking is that everyone feels they have it under control and believes that alcoholism has nothing to do with them. Of course, there may only be a small number of people who start drinking in the morning. But as with anything else, no one starts to drink with the intention of becoming addicted. But addiction begins with the first sip. So, it should really be considered an issue that anyone may face.

I quit drinking about a year and a half ago. Although I had tried to stop drinking many times in the past, I just couldn't do it. I really loved drinking, and I loved bars. But I wanted to quit because I wanted to get up early in the morning, a habit I always aspired to. They say Hemingway always got up early in the morning no matter how late he'd stayed up drinking, so if I had Hemingway's discipline, then maybe I wouldn't have had to quit.

Although you plan to finish drinking after one glass, it's tough to actually stop there. That's because our brain's cooling system, which keeps our desires under control, becomes paralyzed by the alcohol. I wanted to live a regular life, but the quality of my mornings diminished because of hangovers; they never gave me a chance to acquire the habit of rising early. I didn't like repeating that. I wondered if it was okay to have so many regrets in my life.

# Step 3: Leverage turning points

I have now acquired various good habits, but once I move from my current home, I will probably have to redevelop them again. This is because I will have to recreate the triggers of habits that are tied to my current environment.

Conversely, it's good to use a turning point—like moving—if you want to quit something. For me, the turning point in my journey to quit alcohol was an illness.

Alcohol is a drug, and it involves physical dependence. Therefore, it's tough to quit with something simple like willpower. It's the same as being unable to will yourself to stop eating when you're so hungry that you feel you'll die of starvation.

During a trip to Ishigaki Island in Okinawa, I caught the flu and spent most of my five days in bed. I had to cancel the diving that I had been looking forward to. Never mind liquor; I could barely eat my meals. But after spending those five days without liquor, I realized that I had less desire to drink than usual. I think those first five days are the toughest obstacle you face when you want to quit something.

I made use of this opportunity.

For twenty days after quitting, I still wanted to drink, and I would envy those who did. But a month later, I realized that even if I saw liquor, the desire to drink had disappeared. Naoki Numahata, with whom I run a blog, also quit drinking after he was hospitalized for dental treatment. I often hear similar stories about quitting smoking. You may feel down when you're sick, but when you aren't in the same physical condition that you're usually in, you get a chance to quit habits that you've always wanted to be rid of.

Thinking about it now, it was being jilted by my girlfriend that served as an opportunity for me to let go of a massive amount of my things and become a minimalist. When I read my records from the time, I often went to places like temples—I guess I wanted to reexamine myself! Turning points like that will give us a push for change.

## Letting go when you most want something

> *If it's your job to eat two frogs, it's best to eat the biggest one first.*
>
> —Mark Twain

I think the timing was good when I quit drinking. It was January, and in my blog, I proclaimed right away that it was my New Year's objective. The toughest period came first: there were New Year's parties and a wedding. It helped that I had moved to the countryside. For a while, my only mode of transportation was walking or riding my bicycle, and there were no vending machines or convenience stores that I could quickly access. That type of environment helped. At a certain point, I even stopped having the desire to style my hair with wax, something I'd always done. I decided to use a date I had with a lovely lady as the day to quit that habit. It meant that I was able to let go when I most needed it, so I would be able to get by on other occasions.

The same thing applied to drinking. Since I'd reached a certain age, relationships with women always began with drinking; it was indispensable on dates. But once you get through that toughest day, you'll be able to ignore any small desires that might develop in your daily life.

The climax, for me, was at a restaurant in New York, four months after I quit drinking. My previous work, *Goodbye, Things*, had been translated into English, and I went there to give a speech to commemorate its publication. We had a party with the local editor, his wife (to whom I owe much in the translation), and the agent. Celebrating a special thing in a special place like New York with special people doesn't happen often in life. I was able to say no to liquor there, and I gained a real sense that I had completed my effort to quit drinking.

# Step 4: Quit completely—it's easier

The eighteenth-century writer Samuel Johnson said, when a friend suggested that he drink a little wine, that he couldn't drink just a little. That was why he never touched it. In his case, it was easy to say no to drinking, but if he hadn't, it would be difficult to control himself. I can relate.

If you only drink once or twice a week, you won't have to give it up completely. But that wasn't me. In trying to control my excessive drinking, I tried to come up with various exceptions because the idea of quitting completely was so sad. "It's okay when I'm with my lover," "It's okay while traveling," "Friends' weddings are special," "I'll only drink beer from organic breweries or my favorite breweries," and so on and so forth.

Think like this, and the exceptions will only increase in number; they'll eventually become, "It's okay if I'm with someone," or "I'll make today a special occasion." The rules will become complicated, and you'll end up thinking about whether or not something is allowed or if you should abstain. In other words, your awareness is called up—you have to spend time thinking about it—so it becomes difficult to continue to adhere to no-drinking as a habit.

The philosopher Immanuel Kant allowed himself to smoke a pipe just once a day, but it's said that as the years went by, the pipe became bigger. If your rule has exceptions, it's not the best rule.

## Habits aren't about being stoic or enduring at all

People who love drinking make a lot of exceptions to drink because we know that drinking is fun. With that knowledge, abstinence is difficult. If something is fun, the days without it are days of endurance. Endurance is a state where there is no reward. People can't keep doing things that offer no rewards.

A technique for quitting something is to refrain from using words that prohibit those actions. Rather than thinking that you mustn't drink liquor, think: "I don't have to drink anymore." Turn your attention towards the pain you feel when you do drink, rather than the advantages you think you'll miss out on when you don't drink.

When I tell people I'm holding back from drinking, they often tell me that I'm stoic. But that isn't the case. You could say I'm being stoic if I'm refusing a drink even though I'm tempted to have it. But as we saw in Chapter 1, people with strong willpower don't get tempted in the first place. For example, let's say I went to an *izakaya* bar.

- *To drink*
- *To not drink*

It isn't as if I'm choosing not to drink after pondering whether or not to drink alcohol. Instead, I'm in a state where the part where I drink alcohol is colored in gray, and I can't choose that option in the first place. I wrote earlier that when you take the same action repeatedly, the dendritic spine, which connects synapses in the brain, gets bigger. Conversely, if you don't repeat your actions, it takes on a dormant state (this might be the reason why people who have overcome alcoholism often go back to their previous ways after a single drink).

I can no longer remember the refreshing sensation of beer or how good it felt to be tipsy, so I don't have the desire to drink to begin with. At this point, I feel pretty similar to an elementary school student unable to understand why adults drink beer. I used to drink whiskey straight up, but now, I feel nauseated and shiver when I get a whiff of a drink with a high alcohol content.

These feelings are probably unimaginable for people who see liquor as irreplaceable. It's the same as wondering why runners running under the blazing sun enjoy themselves.

There's a theory that the only stress you can relieve by drinking or smoking is the stress of running out of liquor or cigarettes. I, too, used to believe that life would be about 70 percent less fun without alcohol. But clearly, that isn't the case: children (who obviously do not drink) enjoy themselves. Pea sprouts will start to grow again if you clip them. In the same way, you can gain enjoyment again even after you lose something.

## You might as well make a bold change if you can't do it

While we're on the subject of the importance of setting objectives, there's a story I like that I want to share. Matsushita Electric (called Panasonic today) is said to have set up a plan to reduce its electricity bill by 10 percent in order to cut back on costs. This didn't go well. When its executives gathered and discussed what they should and shouldn't do, the company's founder Konosuke Matsushita is said to have said: "All right. Then we will change our objective and aim for a reduction by half instead of 10 percent." An objective of a 10 percent reduction is tough, because it involves superficial techniques. But to cut costs in half, the entire structure of the company needed to change. Then, finally, it could start to expect the desired results. This is similar to my belief that it's easier to break certain habits completely, to quit cold turkey.

# Step 5: Know that you always have to pay the price

*When you look at the size of the things that you threw away or are trying to throw away, you'll see the size of the things that you are trying to acquire.*

—*The Summit of the Gods*

When you're breaking or acquiring habits, it's important to acknowledge that you can't just focus on the positive points. Author John Gardner once said that you'll always pay the price if you break the law, and you'll always pay the price even if you abide by it.

For example, it's very dangerous if you ride a bike without a helmet, and you might get caught by the police. But if you obey the law and wear a helmet, it's safe but cramped, and the sense of freedom that's unique to riding a bike without a helmet will fade away.

GOOD HABIT INHIBITOR:
Trying to focus on just the good points

In the same way, I pay a price for staying off liquor. I don't drink, even in fun situations or celebrations, which makes some people sad. I can fully understand that because back when I was fond of drinking, I thought that people who didn't drink were no fun. The following are some of the reactions I received after I quit:

A friend: "Come on, it can't hurt to drink just a little. Let's drink."

My mother: "I feel kind of lonely."

Golden Gai in Shinjuku: "Quit your useless resistance!"

A French person: "Oh . . ."

Because I love things, I didn't deny their value after I had parted with them myself. There are sometimes misunderstandings when people part with something popularly beloved, such as drinking. The more a person wants to quit a habit, the more they may look at someone who has successfully broken that habit and feel angry. People who are unable to clean up or part with their things will sometimes feel anger towards minimalists, and I believe it's because some part of them is anxious about their own actions. They wouldn't feel angry if they really thought they were doing the right thing.

Even though there are prices to pay for not drinking, there are many advantages, as well: creating a regular routine, improving my health, decreasing my expenditures and trash, avoiding drunken, problematic actions, maintaining a clear mind until the day's end. More than anything, my days are now peaceful, and I don't have to repeatedly deny the temptation to drink. When breaking a habit, it's important to realize whether or not there's something else that you want to prioritize, even if you have to pay a price for it.

Haruki Murakami runs every day, and he writes every day when he's working on a novel. I hear he often turns down invitations from people who are close to him. He says, "People feel offended when I keep turning down their invitations." But when writing a novel, the ties you have with large numbers of unspecified people—your readers—can be more important than ties you have to those close to you, and in giving priority to that, you pay the price of offending them. I relate with this completely.

# Step 6: Examine the triggers and rewards for your habits

Charles Duhigg, author of *The Power of Habit*, wanted to break a certain habit. Every afternoon, he would go to a café, buy chocolate chip cookies, socialize with colleagues, and end up eating all the cookies. As a result, he gained several pounds. I'll explain the general flow of how he broke this habit.

The problem routine itself is clear, that he ends up eating chocolate chip cookies. So, the first thing that needed to be done was to identify the trigger for this routine. As stated earlier, Duhigg breaks down triggers into the following five items:

- Place: Where was he?
- Time: What time was it?
- Psychological state: How was he feeling?
- Other people: Who else was there?
- Actions immediately before he ate the cookies: What had he been doing?

He took notes for several days and learned that he developed the craving at around three o'clock every day He then determined what the true reward was. There were various obvious rewards, like a diversion from work, the sugar in the cookies, building ties with colleagues, and so forth. But by reducing the rewards one by one, he could see what reward he'd truly wanted.

The true reward turned out to be chatting with colleagues as a diversion from work. So, he set his alarm for three o'clock, using that as a trigger. He made a habit of going over to his colleagues and socializing with them when the alarm went off. The chocolate chip cookies had not been a truly necessary reward for him.

## The rewards from tweeting

If I don't take any measures against doing so, I end up repeatedly checking Twitter. It's not so much other people's tweets but rather the responses to my own tweets that feed this habit. While writing this book, ideas kept popping into my mind and I wanted to tweet about them. But if I tweeted all of them and kept checking the responses, I wouldn't get anywhere with my manuscript.

So, I created a note on my smartphone called "Twitter." I would write things there whenever something came to mind. The results were immediate. I thought I was using Twitter because I was happy to see "likes," but a bigger reward was the ability to save my ideas. I was able to gain a considerable amount of satisfaction by simply tracking my thoughts, even if no one knew about them.

It's difficult to do away with the desire to do something, or the desire for rewards. What we can change are the details of the routine. Something that's helpful here is a tally app for smartphones. You tap the button, then the numbers simply increase: one, two, three. It's an app that simply counts things.

If I get an urge to go on Twitter, I ignore it, open the app, and tap the button. I then feel a sense of achievement; it feels like a reward, and my desire stops for a moment. You can cross your legs, pick your nose, or whatever, but the tally app can be used to fix habits. You make it a routine to tap it if you want to do something. And at the end of day, you can gain a sense of satisfaction if you've accumulated a high number.

# Step 7: Become a detective who looks for the real criminal

For many years, it was my goal to get up early in the morning, but I just couldn't do it. There were many possible reasons for this. Because there were multiple potential culprits, I had to look for the true criminal, like a detective. This is how I deduced my "early riser murder mystery."

I kept hitting snooze after my alarm went off at the time that I'd wanted to get up. Hitting snooze had become a habit.

It should have been possible to get up without an alarm clock if I had been getting enough sleep. It appeared, then, that I wasn't getting enough sleep.

I wasn't sleeping enough because I was drinking liquor before bed and thus sleeping late. There was also the possibility that I was sleeping lightly because of the alcohol. Aha! Drinking was my first potential culprit.

No, it could have been the snacks. I couldn't completely discard the possibility that because I was going to bed on a full stomach, I was sleeping longer hours to digest all that food. It was also possible that I wasn't using a pillow that was right for me.

But alcohol still felt like the most probable culprit. So why, then, was I drinking before going to bed? Perhaps there was another mastermind involved.

As I proceeded with my investigation, I came across a diary entry from a particular day where I was regretting drinking again.

The entry told me that, first, I was upset that I couldn't get started on a file that I needed to write. I somehow managed to refrain from buying beer at a supermarket and bought a bag of potato chips instead. But after I finished eating the chips in a few minutes, I developed a sense of self-doubt. Then, I couldn't control the desire for beer that I had once forgone and ran to a nearby store. I could no longer stop myself after the first beer. Next, I went to the store again to buy a stronger *chuhai* as my second drink.

What started this vicious circle was that I didn't write the material that I was supposed to write, which led to me feeling worried. It appeared that the reason I began to drink was that I hadn't taken proper care of the work that I was supposed to complete in the afternoon. That had been the ultimate culprit in my inability to get up early.

It's fun to dig into situations in this way to figure out where a bad habit begins.

# Step 8: Don't make identity an excuse

There are many writers and editors who have layers of documents piled up on their desks. I used to be like that. It's true that they need a lot of reference materials, and it's a busy line of work.

But I discovered that once I tried not to put anything on my desk, it didn't cause any inconveniences; in fact, my work went very smoothly.

There's something like a sense of dandyism among reporters and editors. To do a good job, you have to have stacks of material on your desk. Maybe it's a guise: you want to appear that you're working so hard, you have no time to clean up.

## Geniuses don't wait for inspiration

In these ways, occupations are accompanied by illusions. An author takes his time writing. An artist waits for inspiration.

I heard that Haruki Murakami was once told by another author that "a manuscript is something that you write after the deadline has arrived." You wait until the last minute before your deadline and you forge ahead with your manuscript once you have your inspiration.

As I mentioned earlier, these types of illusions are shattered in the book *Daily Rituals: How Artists Work,* which follows the daily lives of 161 authors and artists. People who are actually active in their fields have very regular routines and habits. The artist Chuck Close says that it's an amateur thought that people draw when they get struck by inspiration: professionals like him get to work when it's time to work.

The composer John Adams also said that, in his experience, the habits of truly creative people are extremely plain, and there's nothing particularly interesting about them.

## Identities can be changed

Not only can you learn to look past the illusions associated with your occupation, but it's possible to change your overall identity.

There was a time when I was convinced that I was a night person, and someone who couldn't live without alcohol. Most members of my family are fat, and when I was fat, too, I believed it was genetic.

In reality, my being fat was simply because I'd accumulated bad habits; being fat at the time didn't mean that that couldn't be changed. Now, as a minimalist, if I were to hold back from getting the things that I really want because of that minimalist identity, I would be getting my priorities backwards. Our present identities shouldn't constrain our future actions.

# Step 9: Start with keystone habits

Among the different types of habits are those called "keystone habits." Keystone habits lead to the development of other habits—like a domino effect.

My keystone habit was cleaning up, which began when I became a minimalist. Once I reduced the number of clothes and plates that I had, I couldn't accumulate laundry or dirty dishes in the first place. I began to take care of the clothes and dishes I did have, and doing so was simple because there wasn't much to clean or organize. What happened then was that I began to enjoy doing household chores, something I used to think I despised. You can develop a fondness for things that you previously hated, under the right conditions. That was what initially prompted my interest in habits. People develop a fondness for things that are easy to do and offer rewards, and can quickly make them a habit.

## Minimalism will lower the hurdle for developing other habits

Because I select things carefully now, I spend less time shopping and managing my possessions. The time that I save is useful for acquiring new habits. And the advantage of reducing your possessions is that it lowers the hurdle for starting to work on all your other new habits.

For example, I was able to make yoga a part of my routine

because my decluttered room made it easy to pull out and put away my yoga mat. If you can't find your gym clothes, you may stop going to the gym. You feel completely different when you wake up in a tidy room than in a messy one. I believe that minimalism is a pretty effective way to acquire other good habits.

If you're unsure about where you should begin with acquiring good habits, I recommend reducing your belongings as a first step. If you reduce your things appropriately, less mess will build up. You'll develop a habit of putting items away after using them.

## Reducing things through exercise

Of course, the order in which new habits are acquired will vary from person to person. Some people will start by developing an exercise routine. I know someone who, first, made it a habit to work out. Once he did that, he looked better, and thus felt that simple clothes like a tee shirt and jeans were enough. And after he began to reduce the amount of clothing he had, he also went on to reduce his other possessions. There are probably those who would like to start with a diet. There are also people like Arnold Schwarzenegger, who began with a habit of working out with weights, and whose career expanded as an actor and then as a politician.

## Waking up early is both the vanguard and the general

Waking up early in the morning is also an important habit. We can't control the number of hours we spend at school or at work, but the morning is a time when we can choose the hour at which we get up. The time after you get up is the time when you can concentrate the best. As the day goes by, unexpected things and distractions will happen and build up, so it's best to do what you want to do in the morning.

For me, it isn't tough to get up early, as I usually get plenty of sleep. But there are times when I wake up in the middle of the night, and then when it's time to get up in the morning, I want to get more sleep. To overcome that, I remind myself that not getting up early in the morning will inhibit good habits. Even though I've been keeping track of my habits to date by writing notes in my diary and on my app, I often skip yoga, a habit that follows getting up in the morning, and my meditation, which I can't do when I can't get up early. As we've seen in Chapter 1, a sense of self-doubt is generated by not following a regimen, and willpower gets lost. Those are the times when I end up lounging around all day.

If you fail at getting up early, all the habits that depend on that one collapse. That's why I began to think that waking up early is both the vanguard and the general. Waking up early is a must, and if you lose that first battle, you will lose in all the battles.

By assigning more responsibility to the act of getting up early, I can now get up earlier. Right after I get up, I get my body moving with yoga, and my head clears right away. With the development of this habit, I fight the morning grogginess with the thought that I'll have a clear head in five minutes, anyway, and can then manage to start my day.

# Step 10: Keep a diary to record observations about yourself

One habit that I recommend starting as early as possible is keeping a diary. It's a record of your progress. I doubt that anyone can acquire good habits without a single lapse just by reading this book. In fact, you can't gain a real sense that there are truly disadvantages to not acquiring good habits unless you continue to fail. That's why we should keep track of our failures. We should keep records of the types of excuses we make for our failures and the types of situations that we were in. That way, it'll be easier to cope when a similar situation occurs.

The psychologist Kelly McGonigal explains the importance of reflecting on the moment you chose your course of action. Through a diary, we can reflect on when we made a decision for the purpose of accomplishing a habit, or how we went about coming up with a good excuse.

## You'll understand your hidden tendencies

Unless you record everything, you can twist the truth at your convenience as much as you want. Related to this idea is the psychological phenomenon of "motivated reasoning," which purports that you first decide whether or not to do something, then come up with the reasoning.

Here's an example: when I started thinking about cutting carbs,

I was at a point where I couldn't control my intake. It says in my diary: "I heard it's more efficient to have the occasional cheat day to eat lots of carbs instead of always staying off them." Because of this reasoning, I set up many cheat days.

My diary also shows that I had been justifying my alcohol intake with reasons such as: "Hey, red wine seems to have a fat-burning effect!" and "I'm celebrating the reprint of my book!" But it wasn't that I wanted to celebrate. I just wanted to drink.

Once I find an excuse that sounds right, there's no stopping me. Unless I keep a record, my memory will be altered as to which of my reasons were actually excuses. Records are ruthless. I've written over and over in my diary that I thought I was only going to drink one glass of liquor, but once I did, I couldn't stop. In keeping and reviewing records, the disadvantages finally sink in. It was an impossible dream for me to drink just one glass.

## A clear marker for when to start worrying about my weight

You can see your hidden tendencies by examining your own diary. I'm five feet, nine inches tall. I start to get concerned about the flab on my stomach and my chin when my weight goes over 150 pounds, and I end up losing my ability to concentrate. Through my diary, I've learned that I always react the same way when I exceed that weight. So, I try to keep my weight under this clear 150-pound mark. By keeping records in my diary, I've learned to objectively identify the point when I start to get into what I used to vaguely call "a mood."

## A tip for diary entries: Write the facts

When keeping a diary, focus on writing the facts rather than writing well. Many people think that writing a diary means writing metaphors and essays filled with lessons. That's tough, and you won't continue to write. It's good enough to write so that *you* understand it, rather than on the precondition that someone else will read it.

I was able to continue keeping a diary after reading *The Magical Power of Diaries* by Saburo Omote. Omote says that, more than anything, a diary is a record. That's why diaries contain facts about your everyday life, like drinking grapefruit juice or smoking a cigarette. The type of wonderful events that you might write an essay about don't happen every day, but trivial things do. That's why you can write the truth at the beginning. What time you woke up, that you ate a combo meal featuring deep-fried horse mackerel for lunch. Even things like these will bring back memories and be fun.

The situation will vary from person to person. The diary that you've been writing will become like a medical record just for you, for the purpose of acquiring habits. You can then formulate a cure to match.

# Step 11: Meditate to enhance your cognitive ability

I recommend meditation as a habit to acquire at the outset. It'll serve as training for cognition—your cool system. Meditating allows you to be meta-aware, which means that you have a sense of what you're thinking and what you're feeling from a third-person point of view.

It means you'll learn to think: "There's a person inside me who wants to eat a marshmallow," rather than, "I want to eat a marshmallow."

It is said that people think some seventy thousand thoughts over the course of a day. Meditation is an act of recognizing that you're going ahead and thinking, and returning your awareness to your breathing. You hone in on the sensation on your skin while you breathe. Air enters through your nostrils, passes through your throat, enters your lungs, and goes back up. While meditating, you become hyper-aware of each area of your body where breathing happens. You'll find that it's not that easy, because your awareness will immediately fly off in different directions. The human mind really starts to chat away. But when you continue to try this, you'll learn to be able to see your emotions and your desires objectively.

Meditating quickly became a habit for me. While this is owing in part to the fact that my apartment was already clean and had an area set aside for relaxing, I think it's primarily because the rewards come right away when you meditate. After I meditate, even the "resolution" of what I see seems to improve. The sediment-like things that were stuck in my brain dissolve, and I simply feel good and clear.

## Meditation and alcohol dependence

Meditation is also used to treat alcohol dependence. It's been revealed that when you meditate, it helps to control the activity in the brain's posterior cingulate cortex.

This area is associated with the act of thinking about the same thing over and over. Obsession is generated through the repetition of thoughts. "I'm a useless human being." "Nothing goes right no matter what I do." Meditation, which gives you a third-party perspective, is an effective method to reexamine such beliefs.

# Step 12: Realize that enthusiasm won't occur before you do something

*The problem . . . isn't that you don't feel motivated; it's that you imagine you need to feel motivated.*

—Oliver Burkeman

Back when I didn't have a habit of exercising every day, I realized that it was more difficult to actually go to the gym than it was to lift weights or run when I got to the gym.

I never have a problem making up my mind to go home when I'm lifting weights. I don't have a problem deciding whether to run another step further when I'm in the middle of a run, either. But before going to the gym, I used to wonder, "Should I go today, or should I skip it?" or, "I don't really feel like going today."

## GOOD HABIT INHIBITOR:
Relying on your motivation

The problem is that you have the preconception that if you wait, that thing called "motivation" will come naturally. Neuroscientist Yuji Ikegaya's words perfectly express why this is a mistake: "You won't feel motivated unless you start acting. You feel motivated when the nucleus accumbens in the brain functions, but it doesn't function unless you start doing something."

Motivation will occur when you tentatively start something. It's tough to get yourself to go to the gym, but because the brain will become motivated as long as you go and start your workout, exercising itself won't be tough.

## There are no regrets when you run

It is also important to note that you won't regret protecting the habits that you have accumulated. I've felt regret a lot of times for not being able to protect habits like exercising, when I'd been trying to acquire them. But I've never once thought "I shouldn't have gotten up early" in the morning, or "Working out . . . what a big mistake!" after going to the gym. If you feel like skipping something, it might be effective to ask yourself: "Will I regret it if I do?"

I think you should follow a similar principle when you're making an important choice in your life. Author and innovator Tina Seelig notes that when you aren't sure about making a judgment, you should weave a story so you can talk proudly about it in the future. No one would want to lend you an ear if you told them about your life and you said your reason for not making a choice you wanted to make was because you were busy, you didn't have enough money, or you were uncertain about your abilities.

# Step 13: Whatever you do, lower your hurdles

To motivate yourself, you must first get started. What do you do to get started? It's important to lower every possible hurdle.

Various physics metaphors can be used to describe the difficulty of getting started.

The biggest force is necessary when a wheel starts to rotate, but once it starts to rotate, not much strength is required to keep it moving. A motor will get a train moving, but inertia can take over from there. The fuel that a rocket uses for the few minutes immediately after launch is greater than the amount used in the eight hundred thousand kilometers to follow.

It's tough when you first start to study a new language because you can't make out anything that the other person is saying, but it gets easier when you start to understand more words. So it's important to remove as many of the obstacles as possible at the moment when you need the most force, and to remove as many of the pebbles that tumble on the road as you can.

## Learning from just how low the hurdles are in the habits that you want to quit

For easily addictive actions, the hurdles are frighteningly low. For example, it's very difficult to distill your own alcohol, but it's easy to drink. You can go to any convenience store to pick up some beer, and all you have to do is open the can. Cigarettes are small and light, too, and you only have to light them and inhale. Video games and gambling don't make your muscles scream or cause you to sweat; you only need to move your hands. Smartphones are the same: they're small and easy to pull out of your pocket, so you come to depend on them. A person opening up and reading a newspaper on the train is a lesser-seen image these days, probably because doing so has become a relatively cumbersome act. The government might be concerned about people's dependence on smartphones in the future and create a law like this: "Smartphones are not to be made smaller than iPads (at their current size, that is)." That said, Yukio Noguchi writes books while lying on a sofa and dictating to his smartphone. He's leveraging the low hurdle of smartphones to do his work.

## How Amazon lowers the hurdles

I think Amazon is number one when it comes to lowering its hurdles for shoppers. It offers us one-click purchases, and it even lets us tell Alexa to order a soda for us.

When a disaster occurs somewhere, I think of making a donation online. Often, though, I get discouraged somewhere along the way by the need to create a new user name and password and enter my credit card number; Amazon would have all that information already. Amazon rules over the buying habits of so many people because its hurdles are extremely low.

## There are three types of hurdles to lower

There are different types of hurdles that should be lowered in order to acquire good habits: time and distance, procedures, and psychology. I'll explain each of these.

First, there's the hurdle of time and distance. It's extremely enjoyable to run around the Imperial Palace. But it's not easy to make it a habit if you have to get on the train and wait an hour to get there. It's easier to continue running if you find a course near you. If you're going to a gym, the most important thing is its proximity to your home. If there's anything that you want to continue doing, the first thing to do is ensure that you can do it somewhere close by.

Next, there's the hurdle of procedures. When I was acquiring the habit of going to the gym, I made an effort to reduce the number of things that I needed to bring with me. One day, I was dawdling around at home, wondering, "Should I go today or not?" I then listed all the procedures that awaited me at the gym and thought about what it was that was holding me back.

The gym is close to my home, and I can get there right away in my car. One thought that came to mind was: "It's a hassle putting on and taking off spandex." It's a small thing, but the accumulation of small things will change the actions that people take. Although I thought it more stylish to sport athletic clothes I decided to wear a comfortable pair of ordinary pants. I stopped mixing my sports drinks with powder and switched to plain water. I also made my gym bag easier to use. Though these were little things, they produced big effects, since the result was that going to the gym became a habit.

Here's some interesting advice on lowering procedure hurdles. Marathon runner Mari Tanigawa recommends wearing as your pajamas an outfit that you can immediately go out in, if you want to make morning runs in the winter a regular habit. Indeed, it should be easier to make a habit of running in the morning if you remove the hassle of getting changed in the cold.

We can't skip psychological hurdles, either. For example, I encountered various psychological hurdles when I went to a yoga class for the first time. I thought, "I might be laughed at, since my body's so stiff," and "What will I do if I'm the only guy there?," and so on and so forth.

But these are the types of hurdles that any beginner would feel. They're also qualms that are addressed in the frequently asked questions of the yoga community. The body can be made flexible no matter how old you are. The stiffer your body, the more enjoyment you can get in the changes compared to people who are flexible to begin with. And more than anything, the objective of yoga isn't to strike poses. Once I got a little used to it, I rather enjoyed the fact that there were few guys around.

# Step 14: Realize that hurdles are more powerful than rewards

Faced with massive amounts of information before our eyes, we're getting more and more impatient. While the bounce rate (or the percentage of visitors who enter a website and then navigate— "bounce"—away without viewing the other pages) for sites that reload within a maximum of two seconds is around 9 percent, almost 40 percent quit looking at the site when the reload time is five seconds.

In other words, regardless of how interesting the content on the site may be and no matter what fabulous products are being sold there, things that take time don't get used.

Even if you decide to keep a diary, you'll fail if Word keeps whirling around and refuses to launch. That's why I typed mine in a basic text editor until keeping a diary became a habit. Because the text editor launched quickly and worked well, I didn't quit while I waited for it to open. Logging the date was easy; I could just type "today" or "tomorrow," and Google Japanese Input would convert it to the correct date.

People's motivation will easily go away when faced with a simple hurdle.

## Deciding to operate or donate
## an organ is also a hurdle

An example that behavioral economics researcher Dan Ariely introduces is pretty shocking.

When presented with a hypothetical case, in which they were considering whether to go forward with a planned surgery for a difficult case, many doctors decided not to operate after all when told that there was actually still one type of drug that had yet to be tested. If they were instead told there was a second drug type also available for testing, you would think that the doctors would then choose to first test both, and then decide between the two drugs or surgery. But surgery was often their first choice when given the option of two types of drugs. Doctors chose to operate when the alternative was another complicated decision.

The same thing can be said for important issues like organ donation.

Donation rates will drop when people are asked to enter a check mark if they would like to make a donation. The donation rate will rise when people are asked to enter a check mark if they would *not* like to make a donation. In short, when people are faced with a difficult issue like organ donation, they will hold off on making a decision and choose the default option.

# Step 15: Raise the hurdle for habits that you want to quit

Because cracking pistachio shells is a lot of trouble, it's easier to avoid eating too many of them compared with glazed nuts. I call this the pistachio theory. If there's a habit that you want to quit, it's important to raise the hurdle, and look for a preventative measure like those pistachio shells.

I noticed that if I had social media apps on my smartphone, I'd open them frequently. So I now look at them on my web browser and log out every time I finish. That way, there's the trouble of the two-step verification of re-entering my user name and password if I want to view a social media site again, and, sometimes, I reconsider with that hurdle in mind.

When I was studying to get into university, I developed a habit to prevent myself from neglecting my studies. I'd sit in my chair with my back to the wall, pulling the desk right up to me. I set it up so that even if I wanted to take a break, I wouldn't be able to get up from my chair without going through the trouble of moving the heavy desk. It proved to be pretty effective.

In various situations, it is effective to limit yourself physically:

- Place your smartphone far away from you so you can't use snooze right away when you get up in the morning.
- Use a debit card instead of a credit card so you can only

use the money that you have in your account, which will reduce the likelihood of wasting your money.

If you don't have a TV in the first place, you won't be able to lounge around and watch it. Gretchen Rubin, author of *Better Than Before: What I Learned About Making and Breaking Habits,* suggests creating interesting hurdles and brings up noteworthy facts:

- Eat with your non-dominant hand to stop yourself from eating quickly.
- *A bank robber opens a safe; all he finds inside are chocolates.* In an effort to stop myself from eating too much I leave my favorite snacks in my car instead of the kitchen.
- The author Victor Hugo focused on his writing by having a servant hide his clothes so he wouldn't be able to go out.
- Some alcoholics ask that the minibar be emptied when they check into a hotel.

## I don't trust willpower!

*I can resist everything except temptation.*

—Oscar Wilde

To construct hurdles like this is to not rely on such a thing as your own willpower. This strategy is based on the assumption that you can't overcome temptation. One can say that this method deals with a person's weaknesses in a calm manner.

The harshest example is from Greek mythology, and recounted in *The Odyssey*. The song of the half-woman, half-bird Sirens is seductive and appealing, but listening to it results in shipwreck and death. That's why Odysseus prepared himself to hear it by having his crew tie him to a mast to prevent him from moving, and he told them, "If I plead with you to set me free, just tie me up tighter."

In the manga series *Ashita no Joe*, Toru Rikiishi did the same thing. While trying to lose weight, he pleaded that he be "locked in a room." But when the door was actually locked, he began to scream, "Open the door!" Toru Rikiishi knew that he would become a different person in the future from who he was at present.

# Step 16: Spend money on your initial investment

I began studying classical guitar last year. Standard beginners' guitars generally cost around $200 to $300, but there are expensive ones that cost tens of thousands of dollars. Of course I considered my budget, but I wanted to pick something nice. The guitar I bought cost a little over $5,000.

One approach to starting something new is to try it out with something cheap, which I don't think is necessarily wrong. But if you spend a certain amount of money on something, then abandoning it would be a punishment of sorts to yourself. By not making use of it, you're reminded of the wasted money that you spent. A higher-quality object, made from nice materials and with good design, could inspire you to pick it up.

Putting quality first is also useful for making something into a habit. When you're exercising, you'll be able to deal well with the tough initial period if you get shoes and apparel that will boost your spirit. Switch to a lovely handmade broomstick, and it'll be easier to get started on the hassle of cleaning the house. Buy yourself an exciting umbrella, and the rainy season will be a little more enjoyable. You can't underestimate the impact of these types of investments.

## GOOD HABIT INHIBITOR:
## Not having the right tools

Manga artist Osamu Tezuka is often said to have been extremely demanding when he was working on something. Anecdotes include him not being able to draw without eating melon, and that he once said, "I need instant noodles from Shimokitazawa." At times it must have been necessary for him to do and say things like that to handle the overwhelming volume of work that he did.

On a different scale: when I began mountain climbing, there were times when I stalled because I didn't have the necessary equipment. It's helpful to prepare tools that will make you feel good—and the right tools are sometimes necessary, just to go ahead and get started climbing a mountain.

# Step 17: "Chunk down"

*The secret of getting ahead is getting started. The secret of getting started is breaking your complex, overwhelming tasks into small manageable tasks, then starting on the first one.*

—Author unknown

When it comes to breaking down your tasks into smaller chunks, these words say it all. A chunk is a thick, solid piece of something. "Chunking down" means dividing up big chunks into smaller chunks.

When you feel that something is a hassle, that means multiple procedures are entangled. If you feel reluctant about doing something, I recommend writing down all the necessary steps. For example, there are various processes involved in starting to go to a gym:

- Buying training wear
- Buying shoes
- Checking the monthly membership fees and selecting a program
- Taking your ID with you and getting a membership card made
- Learning how to use the lockers and the machines

When all these steps are bouncing around in your head, it seems like a hassle. You keep worrying about the same things, and they go back and forth in your mind like this: "I'll have to buy gym clothes and shoes if I want to work out, and as for membership fees, which program should I choose? The machines look complicated to use . . . but yeah, first, I'll have to buy gym clothes." When you start writing the steps down, they will appear more manageable. You'll realize that you've been going over the same steps in your head, and there aren't actually that many to worry about. Even if you can only advance by a day, you'll someday arrive at your goal.

## How to get over a fear of snakes

The psychologist Albert Bandura developed a method to overcome fear in a short period. For example, "chunking down" when you want to overcome a fear of snakes would go like this: If someone were to suddenly say to you, "There's a snake in the room next door. Let's go," naturally, like most people, you'd reply, "I won't go!" Instead, you should first take a peek at the room with the snake through a one-way mirror. It's safe, like when you're at a zoo. Then, you look inside through an open door. Once you get used to that, you take more small steps by putting on thick leather gloves, going inside the room, and touching the snake. When you're able to touch the snake, you, who have always been afraid of snakes, might say, "This snake is so beautiful," and put it on your lap.

Although it may be difficult to jump right into touching a

snake, it's possible to go little by little and take on something that you never thought you could do.

## "Chunking down" to get up early in the morning

The same process applies to getting up early in the morning. Suddenly pushing away your blanket and jumping out of bed are the final results of a longer process of getting up. It's often tough to do that during the cold winter. The entire process looks something like this:

- First, you open your eyes (your body may still remain lying down).
- You pull off half your blanket.
- You sit up on your bed.
- You get out of bed.
- You move away from your bed.

Tell yourself that you can go back to bed only if you get terribly sleepy after taking that step of moving away from your bed. The main reason why people end up going back to sleep isn't that they did so after getting out of bed. It's because they can't get past step one, and stay in a state where their eyes aren't even open.

## How to ask someone out on a date

I like this example of "chunking down" from Stephen Guise's *Mini Habits*: how to ask someone you like out on a date.

First, take one step in the direction that the person is standing, with your left foot. Then, take a step with your right foot. You'll eventually reach the spot where they're standing. They'll ask you, "Why are you walking in such a strange way?" That will be a cue for conversation.

# Step 18: Make your targets ridiculously small

The reason why you can't quit playing fun video games is the strategic setting of the game's level of difficulty. It's easy at first, then it gradually gets tougher to match the level of the progress of the player. It doesn't take much time to obtain a reward for the next step in your development, either.

I remember the moment that I experienced a desire to quit playing video games. It was when I couldn't defeat the boss character that kept making unreasonable attacks, regardless of how many times I kept at it. You only want to quit something when you can't obtain a reward despite your best efforts, not when you obtain a reward and feel satisfaction. In that sense, habits are like crappy games. The level of difficulty is the highest at the start, making it necessary to lower the level of difficulty yourself.

The main reason why you can't stick with something for longer than three days or so is because you haven't lowered the level of difficulty in an adequate way. You make a New Year's resolution, you're raring to go right after New Year's Day, you set several objectives, and you make an effort. Maybe you'll feel like a new person for a few days, but you'll eventually become reluctant to continue obtaining those objectives.

## GOOD HABIT INHIBITOR:
## An awareness of the difficulties

Let's say you set out to do thirty push-ups and a two-mile run a day as your New Year's resolution. The target itself is reasonable, and maybe you can keep it up for three days. Yet sooner or later, you may not be motivated to continue every day, because before you get started, you can't help but imagine the muscle aches of the last two pushups or the heavy breathing of the final stretch of the last run. Naturally, your athletic abilities aren't going to change after just a few days, and thus you become reluctant to get started, come up with excuses, and end up becoming a quitter. Knowing it will be difficult can prevent you from really even trying.

### You might as well do a little more

As I mentioned earlier, the toughest thing to do is to get started. Your brain first gets motivated *after* you've started.

The same applies to tidying up and cleaning house. You have probably grappled with whether or not to tidy up and then ended up cleaning everything once you've gotten started. The Buddhist priest Sochoku Nagai put it like this: "Once you squeeze a rag, you tend to want to wipe that spot and then another spot."

Stephen Guise, author of *Mini Habits*, suggests making your objectives ridiculously small. In order to get started, it's smart to set your objective to do one push-up, even if you have a higher standard that you want to achieve, like thirty push-ups. It won't be hard to start doing one push-up a day, and you might want to do another ten once you're already in position.

## GOOD HABIT INHIBITOR:
## The sense of self-doubt produced by one failure

There are also other advantages to setting small objectives. What's most important in acquiring habits is to avoid feeling a sense of self-doubt. As we saw in Chapter 1, the negative emotion of self-doubt will damage your willpower and have a negative impact on your next action. Set your objective to just one pushup a day, and you can achieve your objective, instead of developing a sense of self-doubt if you really can't do more than one pushup.

When I experience doubt, I make it my objective to simply go to where I need to be or to do only the first step of what I originally set out to do. I often told myself: "I can go home if I really can't get in the mood after stepping into the gym."

Seiko Yamaguchi, who provided the illustrations for this book, shared the following example: "My friend feels down on Mondays and always wants to take the day off. What she does is make it her objective to 'go to the office and sit in a chair.' She can manage to sit in a chair, and it's natural to get to work once she does."

## A diary that you don't want to write in

Actress Ryoko Kobayashi has been writing a diary in a foreign language for more than five years so she can practice that language. She says that, of course, there are days when she doesn't feel like writing in her diary. When that happens, she starts writing that she doesn't feel like writing that day.

Then, the next words begin to come. She can continue to give the reasons why she doesn't want to write, such as, "Because I was very busy with my work."

That's one technique for getting started.

# Step 19: Start today

*Doing it tomorrow is a fool's way.*

—*Operation Love*

When you start doing something that you want to make a habit, you tend to want to start at a convenient time. Your New Year's resolutions are one example. Why can't we make our New Year's resolutions on December 27? Isn't it actually more efficient to start around November 15, when we start to get ideas for the New Year?

## GOOD HABIT INHIBITOR:
## Starting at a "good" time

If we slack off at the office in the morning, we'll likely tell ourselves that we'll hustle in the afternoon or the following day. For some reason, we think that we're already in a wretched state and decide that we might as well stay that way until starting anew.

Seasons are another excuse for putting things off. The cold winter is when things are toughest. We think: I'll start when it gets warm. But when spring comes, hay fever makes things tough. Then, there's what we in Japan call May disease, when people start to lose motivation after the new fiscal year begins in April. There's too much rain during the rainy season, it's too hot in summer, and it's too melancholy in autumn. If you want to blame the seasons, you can continue to do so all year round.

For this reason, we want to start something at a good time: we can indulge in the joy of anticipation if we keep thinking that we're going to start tomorrow or next week. It's this "tomorrow" that's the absolute king of convenient times.

I'll do it tomorrow. I'll do it later. I'll do it eventually. But when we look at it from yesterday's perspective, *today* is this "tomorrow," it's "later" as seen from last week, and it's "eventually" from last month. So, let's start today. Our objective can be small. We can do a single pushup right now.

# Step 20: Do it every day (it's easier)

*To go? To not to go? The answer's decided. It's either go or go.*

—All-Rounder Meguru

When you quit something, it's easier to quit it completely. With acquiring a habit, it's the opposite—easier to do it every day.

People believe it's easier to run once a week than to run every day. This is because they consider the level of difficulty as a sum of the amount of effort each action involves. Because there's a preconception that it's easier to do something two or three times a week rather than every day, they choose to gradually increase the frequency at which they do something. But, conversely, that boosts the level of difficulty. You end up getting caught in a pitfall. Why is that?

Let's say for example that you decide to run twice a week. This is what you'll be thinking: "Was today the day for my run? When was the last time that I ran?" "Today's the day for my run, but as I don't feel like it, I'll make it up by running on three days next week." You'll end up performing a lot of calculations, and then making choices. Then, you'll be stuck tossing a coin to make your decision.

## You don't waver if it's every day

There's no need to beat yourself up about when you should do something if it's already decided that you're going to do it every day.

As you continue to do it each day, it will become something that you *want* to do. Taking action each day is at the heart of the steps required to make something a habit. Perform the task every day until it becomes a habit, and then you can decrease the frequency as appropriate once it becomes something that you want to do voluntarily.

There will, of course, be people who are unable to suddenly start running. In a situation like that, you can start by walking five hundred meters each day. And your objective can be small, like slipping your feet into a pair of walking shoes every day. It's also nice to make it a habit to walk home from an extra train station away.

## It won't become an unconscious habit if you don't do it every day

I have trouble tying new guitar strings, but I don't believe it's very different from tying your shoelaces. I can tie my shoelaces without thinking about it, but I always tie my guitar strings while following a guide.

The difference here is frequency. While I tie my shoelaces every day, I can't learn to tie my guitar strings because I only change them once every few months.

Although I don't usually wear a tie, I think I can put it on without-out forgetting how to do it because I used to wear one every day when I was job-hunting, and did it often enough to keep being able to do it without conscious thought.

## GOOD HABIT INHIBITOR:
## Thinking that tomorrow, you'll be Superman

When we're tired, or when something unexpected happens, we consider doing things the next day. It's funny that for some reason, we feel that we'll somehow be different tomorrow, as if we'll wake up full of energy, radiant, like Superman. We think that our future selves will be able to do things better than our current selves. Credit card schemes use this way of thinking wisely: we conform to the idea that we'll buy this today, but tomorrow, we'll be able to better manage and save our money.

There's an interesting story with regard to this issue. For some reason, Big Mac sales increased dramatically when salads were added to the menu. Apparently, many people reasoned that today, they'll eat a Big Mac, but tomorrow, they'll be logical and choose a salad. People felt more willing to buy a Big Mac with the mere addition of salads as an option.

I've had numerous failures myself, but still continue to think that I'll be different tomorrow, so this is quite a deep-rooted problem. We must keep in mind that tomorrow, we'll do the same things that we do today.

## What if today continues to be repeated forever?

It is said that Steve Jobs continued to ask himself every morning for thirty-three years what he would have liked to do if today happened to be the last day of his life. I imitated him for a while, but got bored of it. When I wanted to acquire a habit, this is how I rearranged his idea: "What type of day would I want to spend if today went on forever?" I won't be Superman tomorrow, and I'll make the same choices that I make today. Today, a day in which I plan to put things off until tomorrow, will continue eternally.

Columnist Frank Crane wrote, as one of his ten daily resolutions, "Just for Today, I will be Happy." "Just for today" is the opposite of "I'll do it tomorrow." It doesn't matter if you don't act tomorrow. But you do it, just for today. And then, you think the same way when tomorrow comes.

# Step 21: Don't make up "exceptions" as you go

While we may talk about making something a daily habit, there are plenty of things that come up unexpectedly. A family member might get sick, and there are also holidays. You might want to forget about your habits and simply enjoy yourself at Christmas or the New Year's holiday. The important thing is to decide on your exceptions ahead of time rather than making them up as you go.

## GOOD HABIT INHIBITOR:
## Creating an exception for the day in question

If you're going to reward yourself, you should do so tomorrow, rather than in the spur-of-the-moment today. You won't experience a sense of self-doubt if it's predetermined, since you will have kept an earlier promise to yourself. When faced with seduction, people tend to think, "I can start to do better right after this," or "It's okay since today's a special day." But keep this up, and your habits will easily deteriorate.

## Consider the conditions that stay the same

Although I love to travel, I haven't traveled in a while as I struggled to acquire certain habits. This is because I felt it was possible these habits might deteriorate in a different environment before they became cemented. Conditions that could change include the lack of a gym, a lack of yoga mats, or the lack of a library. But there are some conditions that don't change. For example, you can still choose the time that you get up in the morning, even when you're on the road. It's a hassle to rebuild your rhythm once you lose momentum, so I make it a habit to continue to get up early in the morning, even when I'm traveling. I also carry around my PC, so I can update my diary. Even if no yoga mats are available, I may simply do Sun Salutation on my futon.

The English historian Edward Gibbon continued his research while serving in the military. During marches he took along his books by Horace, and he researched philosophical theories in his tent. These may sound like impossible actions that only a dedicated individual would take, but we can learn from them.

## Exceptions are important for spicing up your life

After a while, I began to think that my inability to perform certain daily habits during my travels was actually helpful in cementing them. When something becomes a daily habit, you begin to take it for granted and thus start to lose that feeling of achievement that you enjoyed at the beginning. A while ago, I went on a domestic trip for four nights and five days. Even a short trip like that required effort to get things back to normal once I arrived home. Getting to work and going to the gym can feel like a burden. But when you manage to do those things, you experience the sense of achievement that you felt when you first started to practice that habit. In this way, the occasional exception can bring on a sense of novelty and add a little spice to your life.

# Step ??: Enjoy it because you *aren't* good at it

*I'm sure that in 10 years—at least in 10 years—you'll be wishing you could go back and start over again.*

*Start over the future right now. You have now just come back from 10, 20, or 50 years later.*

—Author unknown

Here's a story I once heard: A ninety-year-old woman was asked what she regretted in her life. Her answer was: "I was thinking of learning to play the violin when I was around sixty, but I didn't, thinking that it was too late." Had she started then, she could have played the violin for thirty years.

## GOOD HABIT INHIBITOR:
## Thinking that it's too late to start

I started learning to play the guitar when I was thirty-seven. Sometimes, I wonder why I didn't start at fifteen. I also began running marathons at thirty-seven, and if I had started at twenty and recorded a personal best time, I would probably never outdo it.

But for me, I consider satisfaction to be something else beyond how good my guitar skills are or how fast I can run a marathon.

Whether it's something simple that a beginner does or something difficult performed by an expert, the satisfaction experienced is mostly the same. Joy isn't something that you obtain from results. That's why it's good to start without being afraid. The best time to start is right now. I'm thinking about learning to play the piano. After thirty years of playing the piano, I should get reasonably good at it, don't you think?

You want to take up yoga, but you can't. As mentioned earlier, a typical excuse will be "because I have a stiff body." But yoga is said to be more enjoyable for people whose bodies are stiff. What does that mean? Well, a dancer with a pliant body will, of course, manage the positions right away. But the purpose of yoga is "tying together" the mind and the body, not striking poses.

A person with a stiff body turns their attention to their body and starts to become aware of the voice that the body releases. Nothing is as much fun as being aware of changes happening to your own body. Yoga is something that people with stiff bodies can really enjoy. It might be somewhat similar to me envying people who are about to start reading *Slam Dunk*.

# Step 23: Set triggers

When acquiring a new habit, it is particularly effective to use a habit that you already have as a trigger.

A friend of mine says he does squats when he uses his hair dryer every day. I suggest you get rid of things that you don't need while brushing your teeth. You can brush your teeth with one hand. The three minutes you spend brushing your teeth are enough to walk around finding things that you don't need.

## GOOD HABIT INHIBITOR:
## Not having a trigger

You might feel slightly irritated if you haven't tidied up, but it won't kill you. Speaking English is probably a good skill, but not yet a necessity for surviving at a Japanese company. It's hard to make things like these—in cases where you aren't desperate—a habit. Thus, we need to intentionally create triggers to start taking action.

I study English before I go to work. I feel guilty if I'm late for this "English lesson." That's why I try to get it done promptly.

My *nukazuke* pickles need to be stirred every day, but it's easy to forget to do it until it becomes a habit. What I used as a trigger was looking at the eggs in my fridge. I eat eggs for breakfast every morning, so I tied in the act of looking at the eggs to stirring my *nukazuke* pickles. It's similar to programming. I write in my memory that I am to do X when I see Y. The trigger for my habit later changed to eating *nukazuke* every day.

## "Chain-making": Tying habits together

When I wake up in the morning, the first thing in my field of vision is the yoga mat I laid out before retiring the night before. That serves as a trigger, and I start to do yoga. Once I finish, I sit on the mat and start meditating. And when I put away the yoga mat under my bed, I see the floor, and it's with that image of the floor that I start to vacuum. When I've finished vacuuming, my mind holds on to the image of cleanliness, and I proceed to take a shower. The actions that I take at the end of a routine serve as triggers for starting my next habit. And I tie those habits together like I'm linking a chain. I call this "chain-making."

## Writing a letter to myself

I prepare for the first thing I'll be doing when I get up in the morning the night before. In winter, I set the timer on my heater to a comfortable temperature to make it easy to get up. I'll be hungry and exhausted after I've gone to the gym, so I make a protein shake ahead of time so I can drink it as soon as I get home.

Taking advance actions to prepare for when you'll need a little endurance is essentially a message to yourself to go at it again today, to give yourself a pat on the back afterwards. It's like writing a letter to yourself.

# Step 24: Create an adult timetable

*A plan relieves you of the torment of choice.*

—Saul Bellow (attributed)

A typical trigger is time. Most people probably set their alarm clocks to wake up in the morning, and the sound of the alarm serves as a trigger for the action of getting up

Classes at school follow a timetable. The bell is a trigger for class to begin. These timetables are just as effective for adults. I let my alarm go off, not only when I get up in the morning but also when I go to bed at night. People often struggle to get up in the morning because they don't get enough sleep. Many of them enjoy entertainment before bed, but their bedtime will get later and later if they enjoy it too much. There's a need to have someone, or something, give them a little shove.

When I first started acquiring habits, I charted the bulk of my day on a timetable. I go to the library at half past nine. I have lunch at 11:30 a.m. My alarm goes off at 9:30 p.m. when I go to bed, and it goes off again at 5:30 the next morning.

B. F. Skinner, the founder of behavior analysis, lived his life like it was an experiment. He would begin and end his writing according to his alarm. He used a clock that could measure the total time he spent at his desk, and entered the number of words he wrote every twelve hours into a graph to try to gain an accurate understanding of his productivity per hour.

One day, he noticed that he usually awakened at midnight, which he then started using an alarm clock to control, so that he could use that time for his writing.

## Is it stupid to act according to a timetable?

I'm single, I live alone, and I love my freedom. Naturally, I used to think it was stupid to create a timetable and to do things according my schedule. A timetable is something that a grade schooler creates before the summer holidays. And I don't recall ever being able to follow my timetable as planned. What if I suddenly thought of something that I wanted to do? I would hate to limit my freedom with time—or so I thought.

However, if I don't decide on a time to get up, I'll end up staying in bed thinking about whether I should get up at that moment or if it's okay to continue to sleep. If I don't decide on a time to go to bed at night, there are bound to be times when I get engrossed in a TV drama or a manga and keep telling myself, "Just one more episode." The psychology of hyperbolic discounting is when one chooses the reward in front of them despite inevitable regrets the next morning, so that's to be expected.

## Deciding on a time to surf the Internet

I check the news online and look at social media, but I make it a rule to decide on a time to quit. This is because the Internet is too compatible with the human brain. Friends of mine were tweeting:

"I was looking up the meaning of an English word I didn't

understand and before I realized it, I spent ten minutes watching a video of a volcano erupting."

"I was searching for simple lighting equipment. When I realized what I was doing, I was watching a video on outdoor survival."

The brain likes to flirt. It keeps getting interested in different things, and it jumps to other matters without context. From an English word to a volcano, from lighting to survival. The Internet provides answers to these transitions in what your brain is interested in, so you won't be able to quit unless you have a predetermined time to stop.

## Authors and artists mostly work regularly

As I mentioned earlier, many of the geniuses who are introduced in the book *Daily Rituals: How Great Minds Make Time, Find Inspiration, and Get to Work* have regular routines. Most of them are morning people who spend their mornings doing creative work.

For example, those of you who are familiar with the artist Francis Bacon may have seen his atelier so crammed with paints and art supplies that there's barely any room left. Judging by the atelier and his passionate style, you would imagine that he led quite an uninhibited lifestyle, but his work hours were precisely predetermined. He woke up at dawn and worked until noon. He drank the rest of the time, which might seem uninhibited, but he had a set time to work every day.

In the beginning of this book, I spoke about the pain of having too much freedom since going freelance. I feel that it's necessary, to a certain degree, to discipline ourselves with time. Geniuses aren't people who have worked in a spur-of-the-moment style.

They're people who have diligently decided on and set aside the time to work at their jobs.

## The effects of a deadline

A deadline is a kind of timetable that you see over an extended period of time. As an editor, I was sick of being chased by deadlines and decided not to set up a deadline for completing this book. It was a nice dream, to decide on a launch date and to publish once I finished the manuscript.

Although I believed that deadlines were evil, I've since had a bit of a change of heart. Depending on how you use it, a deadline can either be an angel or a devil. It's like a superior who reprimands you when you need it. Come to think of it, our very lives have a deadline. Because of it, we don't want to spend our days idly.

## Using a timetable to understand our limitations

There are many other advantages to creating and maintaining a timetable. One of them is that it allows you to gain an accurate grasp of the amount of work that you can do in a day.

According to research, people are said to spend 1.5 times the amount of time doing something that they thought they'd need to do to achieve their objective. In other words, we overestimate our capacity. It actually takes us two weeks to do work we were planning to do in ten days. This is another example of an illusion that we can be Superman. It's tough to acknowledge.

Back when I was a busy editor, I thought I could make a lot of progress if I went to the office on the weekends when nobody was around to bother me, but in reality, things often didn't go as expected. When traveling, I pack numerous books to prevent running out, but it sometimes turns out that I can't finish even one of them. I end up creating piles of unread books because I underestimate my reading volume and overestimate the duration of time that my interest can be maintained.

## Making clear the things that we can't do

By creating a timetable and following it precisely, we start to see the amount of effort a task requires, the amount of exhaustion it produces, and the amount of rest we need to recover. We see the level of habits at which we need to practice to feel a sense of satisfaction.

We can also see that as the timetable fills up, in order to add something else, our only choice is to pull back. Though I'm the type who likes to gradually increase my areas of interest, I'm not doing that much at the moment. There was a time when I tried to build a DIY mobile home at the back of a light pickup truck until I realized that it wouldn't fit into my timetable. In the past, I would have blamed myself for being useless. But because I was already working on a timetable, I could see clearly that this project didn't fit into my timetable, and I could prioritize other things.

Working on a timetable means you're making visible the total amount of energy that you have and the things that you're able to do in a day. In the same way that you need to check how much money you have in order to shop wisely, there's great meaning in knowing your limitations. It's helpful to create a timetable over the weekend and to take action whether you're a busy student or member of the working world. In fact, it can even be fun to view your timetable like a child before his summer break.

## Deciding when to worry

Timetables play another big role. When your day isn't divided into hours, the time you spend worrying and the times that you're uncertain aren't divided, either.

If you act according to a timetable, you've already decided what you're going to do within that time. If you haven't already decided the time that you'll spend working, you'll end up worrying all day long about your work.

If you go by a timetable, you physically have little time to worry. This is because thinking and worrying are things that you do not when you're acting but rather when you're idle. It's necessary to worry appropriately, but thanks to timetables, I now spend less time being negative and worrying about the same thing over and over again.

There are probably many habits that you can't accomplish due to various factors. When that happens, you can consider that you're prioritizing X rather than being unable to do something else because of X. Rather than being prevented from doing one thing, you're making the active choice to prioritize another. For example, many people prioritize their children, which leads them to relinquish other tasks or obligations. Thinking that you can't do something because of X will lead to emotional distress, and emotions are what are most important to you.

# Step 25: Realize that no one has the power to concentrate

During the process of writing this book, I once tried to measure how long my concentration could last. I checked the amount of time that had passed since I started writing to when my concentration broke and my fingers moved away from the keyboard. The average time was twenty minutes, and I thought to myself that I was lacking in concentration, but that may not necessarily be the case.

A TED Talk is capped at eighteen minutes. This rule is based on the assumption that no matter how interesting a topic may be, people will only listen attentively for eighteen minutes.

In the Pomodoro Technique, a concentration method, the duration is basically the same. You set your timer for twenty-five minutes, and you concentrate on doing something within that period. Once you've finished, you take a short break, around five minutes long. You repeat that four times and take a longer break every two hours.

Although I try not to think while I meditate, my awareness will inevitably start to wander. That's what our awareness is like, so it's hard to focus for long periods.

Even taking into account the challenges of concentrating, using a timetable will still be effective. Charles Duhigg, author of *The Power of Habit*, sits at a desk for eight to ten hours each day. "I sit at my desk for a very long time, no matter how happy or unhappy it makes me, and eventually, the work spools out." You first decide on a time to sit at your desk, and you don't think about whether it's fun. As long as you're sitting at your desk during that time, you'll eventually return to the task at hand, whether your concentration breaks or you start to yawn.

I decided to not take on the reckless challenge of boosting my ability to concentrate. Of course one's ability to concentrate can be improved, and there may be differences between individuals' abilities. But I've started to think that it's more beneficial to work based on the belief that people don't have the power to concentrate to begin with.

Like Charles Duhigg, detective fiction writer Raymond Chandler also resolved to sit at his desk even if he couldn't write. Your concentration may continue to break at various intervals, but at the end of your workday, you'll tend to gain results, even if they're just bits and pieces.

# Step 26: Take action according to the date

Taking action according to the date is a variation of taking action based on a timetable. Every month, I set aside a day to handle miscellaneous things. While I may have few possessions, I do need to clean up once or twice a month, and this is when I do a medium-level job of housekeeping. On these days, I also sort through my receipts, organize the bookmarks on my PC, and sometimes scan documents. While they don't need to be done every day, chores like these will become a hassle if left aside for a while, making you think, "Ahh, I don't want to do this . . ."

While tasks may not be interesting when looked at individually, they can give you a sense of achievement when taken care of all together. Doing so will eliminate the mild irritation that you normally experience by putting them aside, and it will become an act that supports your usual habits.

## The day that you "settle down" will never come

Like keeping house, we tend to think that we'll do something "someday" or when things settle down, imagining a less busy time when we will somehow have little to do. Having lived for thirty-eight years, I have never once thought, "Oh, I'm settled down now. This is it, this has to be the time I imagined back then." A time like that isn't likely to ever come. That's why it's important to set a date ahead of time if there's something that you have to accomplish.

For example, take the carefully decided schedule of a Zen priest:

- Days that contain a four or a nine are for head-shaving and careful cleaning.
- Days that contain a one, a three, a six, or an eight are for begging.

If your responsibilities and tasks are determined by date, there's no need to think, for example, "My hair's starting to grow. What should I do? Should I cut it tomorrow, or can it wait till next week?," and you can act without conscious thought. It's also good to jot down in your diary ahead of time the day you'll start going to the gym or when you're doing something special. (As I write this, I have also noted in my pocketbook: "Go to the dentist.")

It's also helpful to base your actions on the days of the week. A friend of mine does work he doesn't like on Fridays. On Mondays, such work appears difficult to get through. So he takes care of uninteresting matters when he's in a buoyant mood, anticipating the weekend.

## Cherish appointments with yourself

In scheduling your tasks and responsibilities, it is of the upmost importance to give top priority to appointments with yourself. I recommend making an advance entry in your diary (it's easy to repeat your monthly entries if you use an app).

We should consider appointments with ourselves as plans with our most important friend. Unless a truly special circumstance occurs, we must think carefully about breaking a promise with the most important friend that we have when faced with invitations or distractions. You're full of motivation, and you're setting out to do things that you can't normally do. There's no chance that an appointment with yourself, when you're a person you seldom "meet," would not be important.

# Step 27: Set up a temporary reward

*The wise men stated: "Let a man always study the Torah whether for its own sake or not; even if it is not at first for its own sake, the study leads on to that."*

—Maimonides

Just as with exercise and dieting, when you're trying to acquire a habit, you don't see the results right away, which can be discouraging. Therefore, I believe it's effective to set up a temporary reward.

When I moved, I had to switch gyms. The new gym was open twenty-four hours a day; that meant I had more opportunities to go. In reality, I started going less frequently. For some reason, I just wasn't inclined to go. As I tried to figure out why, the answer suddenly occurred to me. The new gym only had showers, while the gym I used to go to had a big, open-air bath. Without realizing it, I had made it my reward to soak in the big bath after exercising.

## Examples of temporary rewards

On my days dedicated to handling miscellaneous things, I sometimes go to the movies as a reward. The author Mitsuyo Kakuta completed a marathon at forty-three and has since been tackling various sports. In an essay, she writes about the importance of a reward:

"Drinking events, high-calorie delicacies, esthetics, massage. I think that thing that's 'waiting for you once this suffering has ended' is considerably important."

- An ice-cold beer after exercise
- A delicious pastry for breakfast as a reward for getting up early in the morning

The effects of these types of temporary rewards can't be taken lightly. And as Maimonides recounted, as we continue to pursue our reward, making something a habit in itself will seem like a reward. Then, we'll be able to maintain our habit, even without a reward.

## GOOD HABIT INHIBITOR:
Giving yourself a conflicting reward

The tricky thing about rewards is that the more you've gained a sense of the results you've obtained, the more likely you are to relax your efforts. In a certain study, people who had been dieting were split into two groups and made to choose between an apple and a chocolate bar. The first group was weighed, and 85 percent of those people, seeing results from their diets, chose chocolate bars. Conversely, only 58 percent of the unweighed group, not knowing their progress, chose the chocolate bars.

This story hits a sore spot. I, too, am more lax with what I eat if I sense I've lost weight. People give themselves rewards that conflict with their objective when they succeed.

It's probably better to give yourself a reward in a category different from your objective. When I was trying to stop drinking, I would sometimes buy myself ice cream if I was able to hold off from buying liquor at a store. It's like coating bitter medicine in sugar; you combine the habit that you're aiming to acquire with your reward.

While I feel that temporary rewards are effective at the beginning, it's important to consider them strictly as a temporary measure until you feel the actual rewards of your newly developed habit.

# Step 28: Make good use of people's attention

*You make me wanna be a better man.*

*—As Good as It Gets*

It's important to do what you want to do without worrying about how others see you. As I began thinking about habits, I started to realize that the attention of others wasn't something to worry about. Instead, it's something that should be used well. This is the most effective step for acquiring habits.

People tend to judge the rewards in front of them instead of the rewards that await them in the future. This is basic human instinct, but we can counter it by making good use of people's attention.

## Making good use of attention from the people around us

I'll start by offering a common example. A friend of mine says she manages her hair with a lot of care when she has a good-looking hairdresser.

You're not likely to receive results from hair care in a short period. Because the rewards are far off, there are times you might fail to keep it up. Even if we aren't particularly conscious of those around us as people we might find attractive, we tend to take note of their attention. They'll be disappointed if we get lazy with our hair care, and they'll praise us if we make an effort.

There are various things that people will see as rewards, and among them, interaction with others and judgment of others are really significant. Why is it that we are so worried about how others see us?

## Why are we so worried about other people's judgment?

It's easy to pin our preoccupation with the judgment of others to the need to feel like part of a group, a major force for our existence. Because we humans spent a large part of our history in communities comprising dozens of members, we are terribly concerned about our positions and evaluations within those groups. As some people could barely hunt on their own, exclusion from such groups posed a threat to their lives.

Even highly intellectual people strongly object when an anonymous person, who means nothing to them, criticizes them. Criticism on social media is akin to being the subject of bad rumors within the small communities to which people used to belong. They're being "dragged down" from their positions.

People are attracted to gossip because gossip, spreading bad rumors, and dragging someone down offers them a taste of honey.

## Prioritizing the community over the risk of death

Despite potential risks, sometimes even that of death, people will occasionally still answer to their communities' expectations. In 1964, college students throughout the United States applied to take part in the Mississippi Summer Project, a voter registration drive for Black people. But due to the possibility of harm caused by radical white people (three volunteers were actually killed), three hundred out of the thousand students who had been accepted declined.

Sociologist Doug McAdam studied the differences between the students who declined and those who took part despite the risks. First, there were no significant differences in the motivation to take part. Personal situations such as work and marriage status were also irrelevant. The difference was the community that the students belonged to. Those who took part belonged to communities that had expected that they would go to Mississippi.

Doug McAdam noted that when someone had friends and acquaintances in a political or religious community, their social status would have been significantly damaged if they didn't go. They would have lost respect from those who were important to them. Of course, they must have also been passionate about equality for Black people. But that hadn't been all; their desire to sustain their reputations within their communities had given them a push to participate in something so high-risk.

## The only way to achieve results in sports

If you want to achieve results in sports, it is crucial to belong to a team with high standards. The sociologist Daniel Chambliss spent six years accompanying competitive swimmers at their practices and interviewing them. He asserts that in order to become a great swimmer, there is no choice but to join a great team. "When you're in an environment where everyone around you gets up at four o'clock and goes to practice, it will be natural for you to start doing that, too. It becomes a given," he says.

When you belong to a team with high standards, you'll try to keep in step with the group and improve yourself through friendly rivalry.

The same applies to the general public. We can look for a team according to our standards. If you're going to run laps around the Imperial Palace, it'll be easier to keep it up when you find someone to run with.

## Using a social media community

It's effective to use not only a physical community but also a social media community to motivate you. The first time I attempted to take part in a full marathon, I tweeted my intent. That was a pretty conscious decision. I planned on tweeting the results from the marathon, too.

My first marathon, held in Naha, was harsh, with only half the runners able to complete the race amid high temperatures. I got cramps in both legs and my feet swelled and puffed up in my shoes. At the time, I had around five thousand Twitter followers, and the idea that I would be letting them down if I gave up helped me finish the race. I might have retired during the race if I'd quietly taken part, with nobody knowing.

To motivate yourself, you can also keep a "diary for the future." Sometimes, I post on social media that I've gotten rid of something before I actually get rid of it. Then, the guilty feeling of inconsistency between reality and social media becomes a punishment that motivates me to actually complete the action.

## How is it that Sō Takei can continue to hustle?

Despite his busy life in show business, Sō Takei is said to take an hour a day for physical training and another hour for researching things he doesn't know. He is capable of doing so because he doesn't want to disappoint his followers (1.3 million as I write this). But you don't need quite so large a following as that of Mr. Takei.

People have used small groups of tens of people and villages as units of communities, which remains effective, even if you use just one other person's expectations as motivation.

## A community can consist of just one person

Once, I decided to cut out sweet foods from my diet and formed a "sugar fast league." I made a promise with a friend, who had also been trying to stop eating sweets, that we would report to each other if we caved in. We made the penalties clear and easy to understand. This may sound terrible, but I told him, "If you break this promise, I'll look at you like this: humph, that's all you amount to." The same applied if I broke our promise. It was useful to imagine the other person's face when holding back from eating sweets. That friend actually continues to stay away from sweets today.

I've recently discovered a system called "pair reading," in which two people read the same book for a prearranged amount of time, such as thirty minutes. They then discuss the book. They don't have to meet in person, and they can have discussions online. Despite the time constraints, they need to gain a deep understanding of the book so they can discuss it, and they must also organize their thoughts, which makes it possible to read with greater motivation than solo reading.

## Your actions will change if you aren't being watched

The conduct of a person will change to a frightening degree depending on whether their actions or results are being seen.

- A person will correct their posture and mind their manners if they think they're being watched.
- A person will progress in their work if there are people around them, like in a café or a library, and they'll slack off if they're at home.
- It's easy to say bad things about someone if it's anonymous.
- A person can get bad-tempered or sing in a loud voice if they're in an enclosed space inside a car.

People worry about being watched by others. Being concerned about your reputation within a community is human instinct. Although it's sometimes tough to care about others' opinions of you, you can use this instinct consciously to produce tremendous force.

# Step 29: Make an advance declaration

Making an advance declaration of something that you should do is a variation of the method of using people's attention to motivate yourself, and it'll effectively produce results.

When the figure skater Yuzuru Hanyu competed at the Japan Figure Skating Championships in 2008, he placed eighth and made the following declaration:

"Japan has the Olympic gold medal won by Shizuka Arakawa, so I'd like to become the second Japanese Olympic gold medalist." He was fourteen at the time, and although his comments were viewed as the words of a child and weren't widely reported, Mr. Hanyu is very good at using this type of power of words.

I also made an advance declaration when I set out to write this book. I'll admit here that I finally got serious after I wrote in my blog ahead of time, "The topic of my next work will be habits." Creating a deadline is the same thing as making effective use of a community, because failing to meet a deadline causes trouble for all the people involved.

You hustle if you make a public declaration because you don't want people to think of you as a liar or lazy. Without a declaration or a deadline, I doubt that this book would have gotten published.

## Creating penalties with commitments

Ian Ayres, author of *Carrots and Sticks: Unlock the Power of Incentives to Get Things Done*, created a business with the system of making advance declarations. You also establish big penalties for not achieving your goals; for example, if you set an objective to lose a certain amount of weight and fail, you pay a thousand-dollar penalty. It's also effective to set up penalties such as making a donation to a political group you hate if you smoke a cigarette while trying to quit. In Ayres's service, you register the details online and a third party evaluates your progress.

This is effective for issues like dieting or quitting smoking, where you would be happy if you succeeded but aren't faced with major penalties if you don't. With objectives like this, it's important to make the details and the penalties fairly big. Otherwise, you'll end up saying, "So I can quit dieting if I pay a hundred dollars, right?" This system of commitment is advertised by some gyms, who say that that's why they have members pay large amounts of money in advance.

# Step 30: Think from a third-party perspective

*I'm okay with that, but I wonder what YAZAWA would say?*
—Eikichi Yazawa

We don't have just one personality.

As I mentioned earlier, our brain has an instinctive hot system and a logical cool system, and when one is activated, the other is deactivated. We should remember that it's this "parliamentary session" held in our consciousness that guides our actions.

In trying to control your actions, it might be helpful to give names to these two forces, like the musician Eikichi Yazawa does. I'm monitored by the other "me." "Aw, this is a drag, I wanna quit. But what would Fumio say?"

There are a variety of ways to employ a third-party perspective like that.

- A future self who does the thinking

Yoshiki Ishikawa, a doctor of preventive medicine, says that when he's tempted by something, "I have the person that I'll be in thirty years ask me about it." When faced with a choice between going for a drink or focusing on his research, he finds that it becomes easier to choose his research by asking himself a question from the perspective of his future self.

- A person who watches over you

Author Gretchen Rubin says that, when she isn't sure whether to accept an assignment, she ponders, "What does my manager say?" In the film *My Golden Days,* there's a line that goes like this: "Address yourself like an older brother who watches over you." It might be helpful to consider things as if you were your older brother, someone who isn't too easy on you and occasionally gives you tough advice.

- An imaginary camera

"What would I do if I were in the middle of filming for *America's Got Talent*?" "What would I do today if I were preparing for a close-up in *Vogue*?" I wouldn't be lying around or picking my nose if I were about to go on stage in front of judges and a live studio audience. I might be extra-diligent about my skincare routine if we were shooting a full-color spread next week.

- What would a person you respect do?

Billy Wilder, known for directing works like *Some Like It Hot,* had a sign posted in his office that said, "What would Lubitsch have done?" Film director Ernst Lubitsch had been Wilder's mentor. Wilder must have considered things from his mentor's perspective when he got stuck in a script. Mentors change with each generation. Japanese filmmaker Koki Mitani is said to think, "What would Billy Wilder do?"

A person who has a strong sense of faith likely has strong self-control; they probably feel that even if no one is physically watching them, they're always being watched by God. This idea is expressed in the Japanese phrase *"Otento-sama ga miteiru,"* meaning that the sun or God is watching you. Occasionally considering things from a third-party perspective isn't a technique that will change you fundamentally, but it's one way to get yourself to pause for a moment at a difficult, crucial moment.

# Step 31: Quit in the middle of something

When my habits are on track to getting cemented, I gain a sense of contentment. For example, when exercising, I'll feel that I can go on running forever. But if I decide to test my limits and run until I'm exhausted, I know I'll get the impression that running is too strenuous, which will have an impact on the next time I run.

It's more important than anything to continue our habits, so I stop when I think I want to do more. I quit while I'm at around 80 percent. That way, I'll stop the action with the impression that it's fun. I don't practice the guitar or study English until it becomes painful. Because of this, I'm motivated to study or practice again the next day. I don't keep going until it isn't fun anymore.

Muscles develop further when they go beyond their limits and are hurt. Top athletes undergo tough practices beyond their comfort zones, but that lies far ahead, in a future time when we have already acquired our habits. Quitting in the middle of something is effective for developing the habit in the first place.

## Hemingway quit, too

Hemingway also quit in the middle of things. He discussed his work style in a magazine interview once: First, he would read what he wrote earlier. Since he always stopped writing at a place where he knew what would happen next, he could continue to write from there. And with energy still remaining, he would write as far as he knew what would happen next and then quit.

Hemingway was well versed in the difficulty of getting started. So if he started where he knew what would happen next, he didn't need to dwell on the issue. As long as you're able to get started, the brain will begin to concentrate. This can also be applied to business.

Although we tend to want to finish up and go home after we've made good progress, it would mean that we would have to start anew the next day. If you're going to write a proposal, rather than completing it, it's better to stop somewhere along the way in order to get a good start the next day.

## Haruki Murakami is disciplined when it comes to quitting in the middle of something

Haruki Murakami shares that philosophy, and he's strict about it. He is said to quit writing when he's written four thousand characters (ten pages on Japanese manuscript paper). He explained in a long magazine interview:

"I somehow write ten pages, even when I'm at eight pages and feel that I can't write anymore. I don't write more, even if I want to. I save that desire to write more for the next day." Even if he writes six pages and finishes writing a chapter with dramatic development, he'll continue to write four pages of the next one. In summary, he writes by predetermined volume and doesn't quit where it's convenient according to content.

The novelist Anthony Trollope said, "A small daily task, if it be really daily, will beat the labors of a spasmodic Hercules." It feels good to accomplish a lot in a day. But rather than taking the occasional adventure, focus on making small, daily steps, and you'll arrive at a destination that's farther away in the long run.

# Step 32: Don't quit completely

*Each lapse is like the letting fall of a ball of string which one is carefully winding up; a single slip undoes more than a great many turns will wind again.*

—William James

When Nippon Professional Baseball goes off-season, all the players return to their hometowns. But even during off-season, Ichiro alone shows up at the ballpark and starts his training.

"I once tried to take time off. To see if it would help, I didn't work out for a month. Then it didn't feel like my body anymore. As if my body were sick," he said.

Ichiro tried different methods at least once, but ultimately did the opposite of what other players do. He is a true seeker of truth. What's important to him is to not quit completely.

The novelist John Updike also made it a habit to write every day, instead of waiting for inspiration. The reason was, there's so much busy work a writer can do, "You can actually spend your whole life being a writer and totally do away with the writing."

## A boar you see for the first time that year is dangerous

I once heard a story from a hunter named Shinya Senmatsu. In Japan, hunting season is limited to the few winter months. Senmatsu says that, when he faces a boar for the first time in a year at the beginning of each new season, he wonders, "Were boars always this frightening?"

For me, this consistently renewed fear also applies to writing books. I tried to figure out why. When I started writing a new manuscript for the first time in about two years, it occurred to me how tough it was. I learned that it was far easier, and far less frightening, to do something if the wheels hadn't stopped turning completely.

## The work techniques of Anthony Trollope, the god of habits

I earlier gave an introduction to author Anthony Trollope, who is, for me, a sort of god of habits. A post office employee, he was the person who came up with England's iconic red pillar-shaped boxes. He made it his task to spend two and a half hours writing before going to work. He wrote forty-seven novels and sixteen other works while working full-time, leaving behind a sizable oeuvre in the history of literature.

His secret to producing so many works was starting the next project as soon as he finished the previous one. Once, he completed a lengthy work that comprised six hundred pages. A normal author would have wanted, perhaps, to celebrate, or take plenty of vacation time. But because he had about fifteen minutes remaining until his usual two and a half hours were up, after finishing the manuscript, he simply put it aside and got started on his next one.

The senses of pianists and guitarists are said to become dull when they don't touch their instrument for just one day. Some musicians claim they lose three days of practice if they skip just one. Not only is there no improvement when they don't touch their instrument for a day, they lose what they've nurtured. For me as well, three or four days without exercise makes it difficult to return to my previous condition. I get out of breath if I run, and I feel heavier.

I have a real sense that the longer I veer from my habits, the tougher it gets to resume them. That's all the more reason to avoid lapses in between. Your habits are further bolstered as you proceed to move forward with them.

# Step 33: Keep records of your habits

Reports say that overweight people lose weight more quickly simply by stepping on a scale each morning. When they think of
stepping on the scale the next day, they become more aware of
their eating habits. They'll regret poor choices and feel down if
they weigh more the next morning, which acts as their penalty. In
wanting to avoid that penalty, they are more able to control themselves from overeating. We should expect these kinds of results
from keeping records when we're acquiring habits.

## Keeping track of your habits on a smartphone app

I use a smartphone app called Way of Life to keep track of my daily
habits. Those habits are broken down by item, and include "getting up early," "yoga," "exercise," and "writing my manuscript."
The app is set up so that a habit that I accomplish is colored green,
while a habit I don't manage to carry out becomes red. There are a
variety of similar apps, among which Momentum is famous.

What's nice about these apps is that when you succeed several
times in a row, you accumulate sound effects and numbers.

When I decided to make it a habit to write a blog, I was able
to keep it up for fifty-two days. Once you get to that point, you're
motivated to continue without stopping.

The comedian Jerry Seinfeld is said to have marked Xs on his
calendar on days that he could come up with ideas for jokes. A

continuation of Xs becomes linked, like a chain. "Just keep at it and the chain will grow longer each day. You'll like seeing that chain, especially when you get a few weeks under your belt. Your only job next is to not break the chain," he said. Quitting a habit, or cutting off the chain, becomes a penalty in itself and motivates you to continue your habit.

## People's memories are vague

Unless you keep records, your memory can rewrite facts in a frighteningly unnoticeable way. At my local gym, the machines record how many times you lift the weights. On several occasions, I thought I'd lifted them ten times, only to read on the machine that I was still at number eight. It appeared that I had rounded off the number at some point when attempting to escape the tough work. I was stunned. Similarly, with my habits, there are times when I'm too easy on myself if I don't keep records and merely go with the impression that I'm doing well.

I try to keep daily records of my habits. When I've succeeded in acquiring a habit, I'll make consistent entries; it's when I struggle that I need to be careful.

I've been weighing myself these last few years, but there were often times when I didn't step on the scale after eating or drinking too much because I knew the result would be bad. Because I knew the result would be bad, it was a sort of life hack to not step on the scale in the first place. But if you're trying to lose weight, you should weigh yourself every day, even if you've gained weight.

The feelings of regret that you experience, the penalty, will tie in to the next step.

## GOOD HABIT INHIBITOR:
## Pretending something never happened

Sometimes, while taking down records, I remember a misstep I've made, and I think to myself: "Let me pretend this never happened." I make excuses such as: I'm traveling, I wasn't feeling well, etc. You can always think of more excuses for something. The Way of Life app I mentioned earlier has a "skip" function. You use it as a stamp for exceptions, but use it too much, and you'll end up full of skips. Keep a cool head and just keep track of whether you were able to accomplish your objectives.

## A list of accomplishments

During the six months that I was lazing around and feeling down, there was a time when I kept a list of the things I was able to accomplish in my diary:

- I was able to send a reply to a complicated email.
- I checked the price of a pair of shoes that I wanted.
- I took the garbage out.
- I paid my taxes.
- I learned how to peel a pineapple.

People tend to think, "I didn't do anything today," and they feel down, but if you write down your every action, you'll tend to discover that you have handled a reasonable number of tasks and prepared for numerous things. Keeping a list of accomplishments prevented me from getting more depressed.

## Your state of progress will give you a push forward

Your memory can give you an additional push when your efforts are beginning to take shape. A study conducted at Columbia University on reward cards is a good way to illustrate this. All subjects received reward cards, which allowed them to accumulate points for each cup of coffee purchased and rewarded a free cup of coffee after a certain number of points. However, the rewards cards differed slightly:

A.  One card started with zero points, and the cardholder received a free coffee after accumulating ten points.
B.  The other card already had two points stamped on it, and the cardholder received a free coffee after accumulating twelve points.

In both cases, the cardholder needed to accumulate ten points for the free coffee, but those who had the pre-stamped card were, on average, 20 percent quicker to achieve their free coffee than those with the unstamped one. This example shows how actions are easier when people have the sense that something is already moving along—in other words, not starting at zero.

Hemingway kept daily records of the number of words he

wrote and created charts. Anthony Trollope also made it a rule to write two hundred and fifty words in fifteen minutes and kept close count. I mimicked their habits and kept a record of the number of characters I wrote each day while writing this manuscript. In addition to the sense of satisfaction that I'd completed the day's work, there was a delicate feeling of joy, as well. A record of your state of progress also celebrates your victory.

# Step 34: Take necessary breaks to conserve your strength

*You must learn to be still in the midst of activity and to be vibrantly alive in repose.*

—Indira Gandhi

In building habits, it is important to gain a grasp of just how much time off you need to recover. If you haven't recovered by the next day, you'll end up overdoing it somewhere along the way. A small crack will gradually spread and make it hard to keep going.

To begin with, you should gain an accurate understanding of the amount of sleep that you need. By keeping track of how much I slept before waking up naturally without an alarm, I learned that I need about eight hours of sleep each night.

## "Deducting" time

Haruki Murakami spends an hour a day either running or swimming; for him, there are only twenty-three hours in a day. Exercise is mandatory, and the remaining time is divided up for other things. He "deducts" his hour of exercise from the day's twenty-four hours.

In the same way, I think we need to deduct basic things like sleeping, eating, and resting from our twenty-four hours. We first secure those basic necessities, and then set aside the remaining time for other things.

People who wind up in hospitals are often unable to meet their basic needs, such as sleeping adequately, eating well, and resting.

People who are pushed around by companies that overwork their employees may experience a euphoric sense of self-sacrifice, in which their pain is their reward. Even if they want to get away from such difficult conditions, it may be hard to cut themselves off from their corporate communities.

But if they haven't secured time for basic needs as mentioned above, it might be time to think about whether what they're doing is worth sacrificing the fundamentals of life.

## Stephen King's work techniques

Stephen King is a prolific author, and according to his book *On Writing*, he writes in the morning. Once he starts working on something, he writes every day to develop his characters. He also writes on Christmas and on his birthday.

But even though he writes every day, he writes only in the morning, so that he is never fatigued. This seems to be the secret behind the work style of a successful author.

In this way, you need to rest in order to continue doing something. You can't continue to work if you don't rest. And rest isn't something that stands apart from work: it's part of the process. If you're too tired to continue, your work habits aren't effective to begin with.

## We're more creative when we're asleep

The artist Salvador Dalí painted scenes that he saw in his dreams. Robert Louis Stevenson, author of *Dr. Jekyll and Mr. Hyde,* got the idea for the book in a dream. The German chemist August Kekulé came up with ideas for chemical formulas based on images that he dreamed about.

The sleeping brain will sometimes do more creative work than the awake brain. Although conscious thought disappears when we sleep, the brain continues its activities, and the number of calories consumed is no different.

In the past, I used to think that time spent sleeping was a waste, something that needed to be recovered. That's why I envied people who could get by with little sleep. But as we can see by examining dreams, the power of our imagination during sleep can be astounding and more interesting than when we're awake.

This is believed to be caused by the random binding of nerve cells during REM sleep that doesn't happen when we're awake. That's why dreams are so surreal, why combinations of our memories occur, and why our brains produce ideas we could never have imagined while awake.

In a similar vein, while writing this book, it wasn't when I was sitting at my desk and concentrating but instead when I was awake late at night with my mind wandering that I came up with solutions, and I felt the "Eureka!" moments. While I slept, there were things that I forgot about upon waking up, with only a sense of "Eureka!" remaining in my mind.

The brain continues to work without rest, even while we sleep, and it gives us unexpected ideas. Sleep, then, seems necessary not only for the purpose of recovery, but also for creative activities.

## Making things boring at bedtime

I think the reason people like to put off sleep is their reluctance to "give up" on that day. People with busy jobs will want to spend their evenings doing their favorite pastimes: foreign TV dramas, mystery novels, puzzle games. These are examples of things that are difficult to put down; you wonder what will happen next.

Of course, such activities are fun, but if you're doing something too intriguing before bedtime, you'll keep saying to yourself "just ten more minutes" or "I'm just waiting for a good time to stop." And it gets later and later.

I think it's a good idea to make the period before bedtime a bit boring. Reading a book that isn't too interesting, for example. With a short story collection or poetry, it's easy to stop because they have many breaks. A practical how-to book or a book on English grammar can also be broken down by item.

The painter Francis Bacon had insomnia and continued to read old cookbooks over and over before he went to bed. I'm guessing that he needed to read cookbooks to slow down his thoughts, as if he were meditating.

I go to bed at nine-thirty, which is signified by my alarm. When the alarm goes off, it's easy to stop what I'm doing if I'm not too caught up in it. I can thus relinquish the day without any regrets.

# Step 35: Nap (the effects of a power nap are enormous)

*Tell me what time you eat, and whether you take a nap afterward [and I shall tell you what you are].*
—Mason Currey

There are famous stories about busy politicians like former British prime minister Winston Churchill and former US president John F. Kennedy taking naps effectively. In fact, as recounted in *Daily Rituals: How Great Minds Make Time, Find Inspiration, and Get to Work* by Mason Currey, many geniuses took naps galore: Einstein, Darwin, Matisse, Frank Lloyd Wright, Liszt. It appears that stressful work, creative work, and napping are inseparable.

NASA, Google, and Nike have nap rooms and recommend that their employees take "power naps," short naps around twenty minutes long. (Every time I see or write text like "Google also does this or that . . . ," I start to feel restless, wondering if there's a greater need for people who work at other companies to have things like those provided to the outstanding people who work at Google.)

I take a fifteen-minute power nap twice a day as well (the first is when I go back to sleep in the morning, as I'll explain later). I believe that, in the future, companies should be required by law to provide nap rooms. If for some reason I end up creating a company one day, my first order of business will be to secure a nap room. That's how tremendous I feel the effects are!

After Fukuoka Prefectural Meizen High School set up a ten-minute naptime, the number of students who got into the University of Tokyo doubled. According to a study at Université de Lyon, students who took naps between rote learning learned at faster speeds, and enhanced their long-term memory. In a NASA study, cognitive capacities like memory and attentiveness improved by 34 percent after subjects took twenty-six-minute naps.

Improvements in cognitive capacity mean the activation of the brain's cooling system. The subjects' desires cooled, making it possible for them to take actions to obtain future rewards. From my own experience, I believe this is true. I take a fifteen-minute power nap before exercising or taking on a difficult job that requires willpower. I feel surprisingly refreshed after fifteen minutes, and often I have brief dreams. Once the nap is complete, I'm full of motivation.

## What does it mean to strategically go back to sleep?

I have a method for creating two "mornings." I wake up at five, and go to the library at nine thirty. In the four hours following the time I get up, I go to work, write, do yoga, and study English. Shortly after adopting this routine, I realized that I was exhausted by the time I set out to do my most important work.

So I decided to go back to sleep for fifteen minutes. This short sleep session is a strategic act that recovers my willpower. While I make it a habit to get seven or eight hours of sleep, I don't wake up perfectly rested every day, and sometimes I get up at odd hours in the middle of the night. I make up for this by going back to sleep, which leaves me feeling refreshed.

The author Nicholson Baker also uses this method. He gets up between four and four-thirty, and he writes for about an hour and a half. Then, he goes back to sleep and reawakens at eight-thirty.

The good thing about this method is that it's easy to get up the first time, even if you're a little tired early in the morning, knowing that you'll be able to go back to sleep later. I recommend this method of strategically going back to sleep, which effectively creates two mornings.

# Step 36: Rest aggressively

The Sechenov effect dictates that you can better calm your feelings and better your mental activity by engaging in vigorous activity, rather than simply resting and relaxing.

When you're tired, you tend to want to lie down on your bed and roll around, but merely lying down won't change your mood, and you might hate yourself by evening. Not expending energy is not the equivalent of resting. You can rest in the true sense by being proactive in and engaging in an activity you enjoy, like going out and getting in touch with nature.

## Preparing a "coping list"

There will be times when you feel somewhat melancholy, even when you lead a fulfilling life. At these moments, it's good to be prepared with things you can do that will bring on a change in mood; you can thus intentionally deal with stress in your favorite way. I call this list of methods a "coping list."

My coping list includes taking a walk, getting in touch with trees, soil, and nature; starting a bonfire; driving my car; going to the movies. Sometimes, I want to go someplace far away. Even if I'm not in the mood for it to begin with, I can definitely settle down or get an emotional boost by getting away. I liken this to lulling a child with his favorite toy.

# Step 37: Cherish the things that you aren't making into habit

*Continuity in everything is unpleasant. Cold is agreeable, that we may get warm.*

—Blaise Pascal

I am now spending days like they're weeks. From morning until evening, the time I spend working and studying is like a week at the office. And then I go through all the habits I should be performing in a day after first going to the gym to exercise. Once the sun sets, it's like the weekend has come: it's time for a free, relaxed period. It's okay to do anything after you're done with what you need to do that day. When I first started sticking to a schedule and building my habits, I was utterly exhausted, and there were times when I slacked off and played around with my smartphone. The strange thing was, I didn't feel guilty. In other words, I realized that it hadn't been my actions in themselves, but rather the fact that they were diversions I was creating to avoid doing the things that needed to be done that was making me feel guilty. Once I started getting used to my habits, I stopped getting so exhausted, and my slacking off and tendency to look at my smartphone settled down naturally. Now, when I have free evenings, I often watch movies.

Anyone would want to use their time as beneficially as possible, and that's what habits are for. But it's impossible to make all twenty-four hours beneficial, and, what's more, it's not necessary. As I continued on with my habits, I started to realize that it was also necessary to consciously give myself time to clear my head.

## Kojin Karatani and Immanuel Kant's ways to take a breather

The critic Kojin Karatani, who I feel is an exemplary Japanese intellectual, ceases to work by the evening and spends his nights watching TV dramas and movies. In other words, he doesn't use his head in the evening. And he's said to have been living like that for more than a decade.

The philosopher Immanuel Kant was also like a god of habits. He famously took walks at three-thirty every day. Because he was always so punctual, people who saw him adjusted their watches. Kant stayed single throughout his life, lived in his hometown, Königsberg, and apparently never noticed that the sea was only a few hours away.

Although it sounds like Kant was an eccentric genius, he actually possessed a social side and was good at conversation. He ate one meal a day, but he enjoyed small talk, not only with his colleagues but with townspeople with various backgrounds, during that meal. He said it was unhealthy for a philosopher to eat a meal alone. Conversing was his method of resting his mind.

## We need changes in our habits, too

In certain cultures, people walk trails for thousands of kilometers. For them, since they walk day in and day out, the walk isn't a trip anymore and it becomes instead an everyday occurrence. Even trips on foot in the great outdoors will gradually become an everyday activity if done regularly. Similarly, when I became a freelancer, my "every day is a Sunday" situation quickly lost its glamour. I began to think that we also need an adequate amount of change in our habits.

It's good to practice your habits every day, until you start to gain a sense of their rewards and then acquire those habits. But more than anything, you want to still feel like you want to continue with those habits. So you can make changes now and then, and take breaks, so that you don't get bored; in my case, I've started to think that it's a good idea to take a day off or go somewhere at least once a week.

# Step 38: Don't mix up your "objectives" and your "targets"

*Success is a consequence and must not be a goal.*
—Gustave Flaubert

According to Bob Schwartz's *Diets Don't Work*, only ten out of two hundred people succeed in dieting, and only one of those ten can continue to maintain their achieved weight. Although there may be many people who achieve their objectives, it's rare to be able to maintain them.

This is probably because many people consider dieting a means to achieve their target weight through discipline, for a set period of time. Once they achieve their target, they're satisfied, and relax their efforts. Eventually, they return to their initial weight. Dieting isn't like obtaining a medical license or passing the bar exam, which, when obtained or successfully completed, doesn't require updating. Dieting isn't a one-time event. The objective of a diet is to find a lifestyle that is sustainable without suffering.

## The result will be burnout if you only have a target

Many athletes become depressed after competing in the Olympics. Similarly, some astronauts also become dispirited after their space journeys.

Professional video game player Daigo Umehara says he experiences the same thing. He's learned to make his objective "continuing his development," not just winning tournaments. He gets burned out and can't go on if his only goal is to win.

## Schwarzenegger's "master plan"

The Japanese terms for targets, objectives, and benchmarks use similar characters, and it gets confusing. To make up for this confusion, we can look at what Arnold Schwarzenegger calls a "master plan."

He continually asks himself: "What is it that I can do today for my big objective, my master plan?"

My target is to achieve a certain time for my marathons. Setting a goal of three hours and thirty minutes sustains my drive to train each day. The overall purpose of running, for me, is to maintain a healthy mind and body. It's also a target of mine to publish books, for which the objective is to fulfill my curiosity.

# Step 39: Look only at the targets in front of you

*A hero is a man who has done what he can.*

—Romain Rolland

In bowling, a common tip is to aim the ball not at the pins but at the nearby arrows. We should keep this in mind when making something a habit. Why is that?

## GOOD HABIT INHIBITOR:
## The "single-coin" issue

Sometimes, a person working towards a goal will suddenly realize the total amount of effort necessary to achieve it, which can be discouraging. For example, to save up a million dollars, one must diligently and patiently save smaller increments daily. But when you see someone who already has a million dollars, the few dollars you try to save appear silly.

You feel similarly bitter when hearing a bilingual speaker's flawless English, which makes it seem meaningless to memorize a single English word.

You look at everybody's projects and accomplishments on social media, and lose motivation upon realizing how much more effort it will take you to reach that point.

## How Kazu played to the age of fifty-one

To deal with the "single-coin issue," you need to focus only on the target in front of you.

Kazuyoshi "Kazu" Miura continues to play soccer at age fifty-two, but I don't believe it was always his goal to play until such a mature age. The idea of retirement had already entered his mind when he was thirty. He thought then that he'd quit in two years, and kept having the same thought every two years until he reached his current age.

My second marathon was a tough one; I injured a knee. Thinking of how much I had left to run at the twenty-kilometer halfway point or the thirty-kilometer point would have made me want to give up. So, during the second half, I said I'd stop after two more kilometers. I kept thinking the same thing after every two kilometers I ran, and somehow reached the finish line.

The film *Hacksaw Ridge* is based on a true story of a combat medic who single-handedly saved the lives of seventy-five wounded soldiers. The lead character remains at the site of his deployment even after his unit has retreated and continues to carry the wounded who have been left behind. Amid the gunfire on the battlefield, all he thought was: "Lord, please help me get one more."

On the other hand, you can also receive courage and motivation from the things you've achieved in the past. Marathon runner Naoko Takahashi once noted: "How much of a distance have I run to date? I only have forty-two kilometers to go."

# Step 40: Experience failures— they're indispensable for your habits

To acquire habits, it's necessary to experience as many failures as possible. Unfortunately, you won't be able to acquire habits simply by reading this book; you need both trial and error.

"How can you succeed?" This is a question that often asked in self-help and business books, and the answer is very easy. Rather than aiming to succeed, you should quickly experience as many failures as you can. Why is that?

A friend of mine says he grins every time he fails at something. To him, failing is discovering a method that won't work, and it brings you one step closer to succeeding. Find many methods that don't work and one day, you'll find a method that does. Seen this way, failure is almost the same as success. In the same manner that work is complemented by rest, success and failure are mostly the same concepts within the same process. All we're doing is drawing the line for apparent results at a particular time and assigning them different names.

No one wants to needlessly fail. That's why we seek advice and hunt for tips. When we do that in order to avoid failure altogether, though, we end up taking the longer route towards success. It's embarrassing to fail, and we may never receive our reward and end up losing out. We might lose our motivation and become unable to keep going. But those who succeed are those who don't quit in the face of failure, and they're the ones who continue until the end. That's all there is to it.

## The meaning of accumulating failures

When something becomes a habit, we're able to practice that habit much more easily than we could have imagined before we acquired it. But that doesn't simply mean you enjoy doing it. There will be times when you're sleepy in the morning, and there will be times when you don't feel like going to work or going out for your run.

But you can overcome such feelings if you keep records of the failures that you accumulate. I feel down when I can't get up in the morning. Like I wrote earlier, it makes me unable to do yoga or my morning work.

A failure I've repeated over and over again is drinking too much, wasting the next morning and the rest of the day, and regretting it. Each time I've done that, I've taken notes. Thinking back, I see them as necessary failures. A failure or two isn't a penalty. As I said earlier, the "you" of tomorrow always looks like Superman, and can act differently from the "you" of today. When you fail and let go of the illusion that you can do everything right now, everything begins.

## Differentiating between failure and self-doubt

With failure, it's important to not become depressed afterwards. Recall the children unable to wait for their second marshmallow in the marshmallow test. It'll get tougher to obtain our future reward if we feel down or hopeless in the present. Let's try not to fall into a trap of vicious cycles.

The more negative something is, the more we tend to emphasize its role in our lives, a natural human tendency called negativity bias. Because of negativity bias, we can't help but pay attention to a habit we've failed to acquire. At times like this, it's also important to turn our attention to habits that we've succeeded in acquiring.

The minimalist Seiko Yamaguchi says that when her house is a mess, rather than fixating on her messy home and feeling disappointed, she acknowledges herself with a statement such as: "I'm hustling so much right now that I can't even start cleaning house!" When you fail at something, it only means the method that you've tried wasn't the right one, not that you are to blame.

# Step 41: Stop worrying about how long it will take for something to become a habit

How long do you have to continue to do something for it to become a habit? This question probably crosses everyone's mind. One famous answer is "twenty-one days." This seems to be a myth stemming from a story about a patient whose arms and legs were amputated who took twenty-one days to get used to that state.

In any case, for something to become a habit, a change must actually occur in the neural circuit indicating a difference in what someone perceives to be a reward. The idea that a complicated process like that can be summed up with a specific number of days is peculiar in the first place.

One paper reported that the average number of days for actions like drinking water or doing squats to become habits was sixty-six days. But this was an average of a range of time periods from eighteen to two hundred and fifty-four days, with so great a variance that it can hardly serve as a reference.

I believe that it's better to not assess habits numerically. Although there's value in challenges taken with a specific number of days in mind, such as a thirty-day squat challenge, the important thing isn't the short-term target; it's whether you'll be able to continue on the thirty-first day, after you've completed your challenge. If, at that point, you're still thinking of your challenge as an act of endurance, you're not likely to continue the habit.

## You'll know when something becomes a habit

There's no answer to the question of how many days it will take for something to become a habit. But I can say that when you acquire a habit, you'll be able to sense it.

I'd like to give you an example of a time I gained that sense. I had been going to the gym for almost ten years, but only once a week or even once a month when I was busy. On the fifth day after I started going every day, the gym was closed. Before, I probably would have been relieved, thinking, "It can't be helped if they're closed. Lucky me." But on that day, I thought, to my own surprise: "Oh, they're closed. What a shame."

My brain was starting to see exercise as something that felt good, something that gave me a sense of achievement rather than as a taxing obligation, which it had been before.

## Signs for a sugar fast

I also know when I've been able to break a bad habit that I wanted to quit. One day, about three weeks after I started my sugar fast, I saw fluffy cream-filled breads, and sandwiches with whipped cream and sweet bean paste, at a bakery shop, and found that I thought nothing of them. I had been hungry, but upon seeing the excessive sweetness, I even felt a bit nauseated. I hear that Japanese sweets are popular among foreigners because they aren't too sweet, and the sensation I got then might be similar to the way a

Japanese person feels when they're in a foreign country and eat desserts that are too sweet.

In the past, I would have had to exercise willpower to prevent myself from eating what I wanted. But my neural circuit that craved sweets seemed to have gone dormant, and today, I have lost the sense that I'm "staying away" from sweets. That's a sign that I've completed the process of quitting them and kicking that habit aside.

There's a saying that particularly resonates with me: "Live the answer." You don't know how many days it'll take for something to become a habit. But when you have the answer to that, you're already living it.

## The goal is to stop being conscious of it

I think every aspiring minimalist's goal is to stop being conscious of the fact that they're practicing minimalism. That is, the goal is reaching a state where minimalism is present in your actions without your being aware of it.

It's the same with habits: once you stop thinking about the habit, you've really acquired it. Regarding the habits I've developed, I don't have a particular awareness of keeping them up or dedicating conscious thought to persevere; I simply act.

I don't have a desire to write about my habits on social media and make people aware of them. Running ten kilometers a day has now become natural for me, not something to be celebrated or publicized. Sometimes I don't feel like going to the gym, but while I entertain such thoughts, I somehow always end up going.

You haven't acquired a habit yet if you're worried about breaking it. When you've truly acquired a habit, you're confident that you would never quit, despite potential situations that might make it difficult to keep it up. Think about brushing your teeth: you feel uncomfortable if you don't. When you're maintaining an action without being aware of nurturing a habit, that might be the time that it has become a true habit.

# Step 42: Do it; it's better than not doing it

In Haruki Murakami's book *What I Talk About When I Talk About Running*, he tells the story of when he interviewed Olympic runner Toshihiko Seko:

> I asked him, "Does a runner at your level ever feel like you'd rather not run today, like you don't want to run and would rather just sleep in?" He stared at me and then, in a voice that made it abundantly clear how stupid he thought the question was, replied, "Of course. All the time!"
>
> I wanted to hear that answer directly from Mr. Seko. Whether despite a difference like heaven and earth in our muscular strength, the amount of exercise that we get, and motivation, he had ever felt the same way that I have when he got up early in the morning and tied his shoelaces. And the answer Mr. Seko gave at the time gave me genuine relief, that, it's the same for everyone after all.

There are times that Murakami, who has been running practically every day for more than twenty years, doesn't want to run. In the same way that Murakami was relieved by Seko's words, I, too, was relieved by Murakami's words.

While habits refer to actions that we perform with barely a thought, we can't always make choices without thinking; conflicts will always, eventually, arise. Because we're human, there will always be times when we simply aren't in the mood to do something.

There is suffering in continuing to practice habits. But compared to the regrets we have when we don't practice them, I think it's far better to do them. By accumulating failures in our attempts to do something, we will someday gain a greater amount in rewards. If we don't make the attempt, we'll have the same regrets anyway, and we'll also have a sense of self-doubt. So we can choose whichever seems to be even slightly better: doing the task at hand, even when we don't want to.

# Step 43: Gradually increase the level of difficulty

Sometimes, you'll get bored of a habit you keep practicing. For example, you get up early, do yoga, exercise . . . and the refreshing feeling and sense of achievement you got at the beginning can seem to gradually fade away.

When your standards of difficulty are too high, your brain will acknowledge them simply as suffering, and you won't be able to continue. But you also won't be satisfied if your standards are too low, and again, you'll get bored. When you give yourself stress, an adequate amount of cortisol, a stress hormone, will be released to give you a sense of satisfaction. There's no joy where there's no stress.

I once asked an instructor at my gym when I should lift heavier weights, and the answer was: "when you're able to lift them up with ease." You also one day find that you can drive a car as you hum, without conscious thought. In running, with more practice, you'll be able to think about something else while running at a speed that had previously exhausted you. The point at which something that used to be tough becomes easy is the point at which you should increase the level of difficulty.

The psychologist Mihaly Csikszentmihalyi came up with the idea of the state of flow, a state where people are so focused that they forget the passage of time and feel satisfaction. That happens when you're taking on something that's just the right level of difficulty, neither too strenuous nor too easy As I write this manu-script, my concentration breaks when I hit logical disconnects or when I'm writing a specialized, complicated part. When I'm writing about something with just the right level of difficulty, a topic that I have experienced and understand well, I can focus and write while forgetting the passing of time.

## Finesse your habits so naturally that you won't notice their level of difficulty

Of course, you won't be able to continue practicing a habit if you increase the level of difficulty too much at once. Rather, you should increase the level of difficulty gradually.

If your goal is to eventually get up an hour earlier, first set your timer five minutes earlier. It's tough to get up an hour earlier than you did yesterday, but it isn't so hard if it's five minutes. Get up five minutes earlier every morning for twelve days, and you'll be able to get up an hour early.

When I run on the treadmill, I extend my time by a minute since the last time I did it, and sometimes increase my speed by 0.1 kilometers each minute that I run. Increase the level of difficulty bit by bit, and you'll improve without failing.

## "Intentional practices" are necessary for development

Ichiro is said to have given himself a different challenge for each pitched ball when he was at bat. Even if he made a hit, he wouldn't be satisfied if he didn't achieve his target.

The professional video game player Daigo Umehara also says, "You don't get skilled at all regardless of the long hours you play without thinking." It seems that simply being hell-bent on prolonging the time spent practicing isn't going to produce results. Take making shots in basketball. Improving your shots isn't a matter of simply throwing a lot of shots, but instead fine-tuning each shot in regard to distance, the ball's trajectory, your wrist movement in the follow-through, etc. You hypothesize and continue to make corrections. These methods are called "intentional practices."

When something becomes a habit and becomes easy, you might continue to practice it aimlessly at the same difficulty level. Dopamine is released when you feel novelty, and neural binding occurs when you leave your comfort zone.

So even if you're consistently practicing the same habits, you might not obtain the necessary stimulation for development. Stretch your legs wider than usual in yoga. Try hustling anew at your job at times you would normally want to quit. There's room for growth when you take just one step further to move forward even when you think you've worked hard enough.

# Step 44: Overcome each challenge along the way

No matter how well you think you've acquired a habit, there will be moments when you just can't get in the mood. The counter-measure is to maintain the minimum.

Stephen Guise, author of *Mini Habits: Smaller Habits, Bigger Results*, suggests that even if something has become a habit, you should never aim too high when you set your goals. A goal for doing pushups can remain one push-up, even if you can now do a hundred. Even if it has become a habit to write in a diary or a blog, and you're able to write a thousand words a day, your objective can remain unchanged from when you first started at one hundred words a day. You can achieve that one push-up or hundred words when you just can't get in the mood to do more.

As I've said many times, what reduces your willpower is a sense of self-doubt. That negative feeling of not being able to work on something today or not being able to achieve your objective will make it tough to proceed to your next habit. It's important, then, to maintain a baseline for your habits, to avoid denying yourself the satisfaction of completion. Even if you weren't able to do much today, you can make up for it tomorrow.

## Your development will not serve as motivation

*The biggest reward for a thing well done is to have done it.*
—Voltaire

Even if you continue to practice your habits, you'll only feel a sense of development every now and then; it won't be possible to keep the habit up if you consider that your sole reward, or use it as your motivation.

Take yoga, for example. My body became more flexible right away, about two weeks after I started, and I was happy and eager to continue. But, eventually, my flexibility stopped improving, even when I continued to practice yoga every day. Even with a sense of your development, questions like "Will my hamstrings be more flexible today than usual?" will sneak up very, very quietly. I've been following a guide for doing the splits in a month for more than six months, but I still can't do it at all.

I won't want to continue at times like this if I expect development as my reward. And my body will become stiff if I don't practice yoga for a few days, and I'll feel like a failure. English is the same. There are days when suddenly, I can understand what English speakers are saying, but generally, I'm at a place where I feel no development. Development is accompanied by periods of stagnation and breakthroughs. Rather than a straight line that continuously climbs upwards, it's a zigzag, like going up and down a stairway. So if I value development as a reward, I'll want to quit at periods of stagnation.

In order to continue, it's necessary to look for a reward in the actions themselves rather than your own development. You should set self-approval as your reward for being able to persevere with your habit again today. This is really important. At moments of stagnation, it might be good to imagine yourself as a chrysalis. The exterior appearance of a chrysalis will never change. But inside, preparations for the next stage are steadily under way. The joys of development are like bonuses received from a company that doesn't seem to be doing too well. Consider yourself lucky to receive them every now and then.

# Step 45: Keep at it, and increase your self-efficacy

*All you need in this life is ignorance and confidence, and then success is sure.*

—Mark Twain

In Step 17, I introduced to you a way to overcome a fear of snakes by "chunking down," or breaking the task down into smaller steps. There's more to that example. Interestingly enough, people who were able to overcome their fear of snakes were also able to overcome other fears. After earnestly tackling one thing, they were no longer so easily dejected, even when faced with failure. Psychologist Albert Bandura called this "self-efficacy."

Put simply, to have a sense of self-efficacy is to believe, "I can do it!" It's the belief that you can change, grow, learn, and overcome new challenges.

I quit eating sweets after I quit drinking, and this is what I thought at the time: "I could quit liquor, so there's no way I couldn't quit sweets!"

When you succeed at something, you feel that your next success is in reach. Children who were able to wait for two marshmallows in the marshmallow test may have already had many experiences of overcoming challenges, and receiving praise for doing so, by the time they were four or five.

On the other hand, if you think "I can't do it" or "I fail at everything I try to do," it would be a rational decision to give up as soon as possible when faced with a new challenge. If you think that you'll fail again, anyway, you'd consider it a waste of time to deal with your conflicting emotions. Rather than trying to wait as long as you can to eat the marshmallow in front of you, in hopes that you'll later be rewarded with two marshmallows, you'll end up arriving at the decision that it would be best to eat one marshmallow now as soon as you receive it.

This is what Walter Mischel says: Children who have bigger expectations for success will have more confidence when they're given a new challenge, as if they have already succeeded. They don't believe they'll fail, and so they wish to face it head-on, and choose to take the risk of failure.

When you're starting something new, people advise that you should "just do it," and I agree. But the people who are able to "just do it" are those who have many experiences of just doing it and things somehow working out.

That means it'll be easy for you to take on new challenges if you aren't afraid of failure, and you'll continue to succeed.

## A sense of self-efficacy that began with cleaning up

Children who were able to wait in the marshmallow test were often "successful" by other measures too, like their test scores and their states of health.

I think it's a result of the sense of self-efficacy—"I can do it!"—that extended to various aspects of their lives.

I can say that that applies to me, too. I began by cleaning my apartment, but it wasn't enough; I developed a desire to improve my life in various other ways. I learned to get up early in the morning, and there was initially such a great sense of accomplishment when I made it to the gym that I felt satisfied even if I slacked off afterwards. When you become able to get up early and exercise with ease, you start to want more challenges.

When you acquire one habit, you want to acquire other habits as well. Because your sense of self-efficacy has been boosted by developing that one habit, it becomes easy to form the next habit. And, in that way, the positive impact extends beyond that initial habit.

# Step 46: Create a chain reaction

It took a while for exercise to become one of my habits. After I moved to the countryside, I either ran or drove a car. When I walked a long distance for the first time in a while, I was surprised to see how quickly and steadily I was able to walk. There was a sensation like my legs and hips were more compact. My body felt light, like when Goku, in *Dragon Ball*, takes off his weighted clothes.

People who can only walk slowly are said to have various health risks, like depression and declining bodily and cognitive functions. Shouldn't you be able to walk briskly when your body feels light and you feel motivated?

You daily life becomes really easy when you start to condition your body. The fatigue from climbing stairs becomes practically zero, so there's no need to choose the crowded escalator. You don't get out of breath. And furthermore, your health doesn't decline.

## The habits you've already acquired become your reward

Because you'll have started different habits at different times, there will be habits you've already acquired that now have a low rate of difficulty and are fun. For me, one example would be writing in my diary. I no longer have any trouble writing in my diary. I can write about negative feelings, and things will start to brighten up right away. For me, writing in my diary is a way to refresh myself, and it's also a reward.

Running is the same. I used to think, "I'll eat something good if I can accomplish this run," but I've realized that somewhere along the way, I started thinking, "I'll go running when I finish this work." A habit that used to be a challenge has now become a reward, and a practice that's indispensable for me.

## You'll no longer need bad habits

Even if I'm plagued with some type of stress, I'll feel better when I write it down in my diary. Even when I'm feeling bad, my mood will definitely improve if I go for a run. There's no more need for me to eat or drink too much, or to go shopping on a whim, which I previously believed were ways to relieve stress. In these ways, positive actions reinforce one another. "He's stoic," "He has strong willpower"—it only looks that way when other people see me doing these things.

# Step 47: Adapt your habits as needed

*All our life . . . is but a mass of habits.*

—William James

The ways to approach habits that we've covered in this book can be applied to various aspects of our lives. For example, I have a habit of eating very quickly, and although I wanted to correct that, it wasn't easy to do. When I'm having a meal with a woman, there is a considerable difference in our eating speeds if I'm not careful.

It's important to eat slowly in order to control our appetite, and it's also good for digestion. I know I should slow down, but it's hard. What I need in order to develop a habit are penalties and rewards. So I applied that principle. I set up a rule where I allowed myself to only take a break while I ate my lunch. In other words, if I finished my lunch quickly, the penalty was that I had that much less time to rest, and if I ate slowly, there was the reward of taking a longer, relaxing break. The results weren't tremendous, but I think there was some improvement.

Many people don't take their prescribed medication, even though the reward for doing so is that it improves your health, because often it's hard to see a positive effect right away. So it's hard to make it into a habit, and it's easy to forget to do. To remember to take your medication, it's good to use something that you do every day as a trigger, as I've mentioned before. It's effective to leave the medication by your hair dryer if you use that every day, or close to your toothbrush.

## Meal habits, money habits

For me, meals are also a habit. I cook three meals a day, and the menu lineup is the same. My routine is to go to the supermarket once every three or four days, buy the same items, and cook in the same way. This way, I eat basically the same quantity every day, so I don't overeat with "I've made too much and I'm going to waste the food" as an excuse. Eating out and enjoying tasty dishes is fun, of course, but a stable diet also has the advantage that you can't gain weight.

Habits can also be used to govern big issues, such as money. From the standpoint of the Japanese inclination to save money, Americans seem to have very small savings. According to a 2016 study of seven thousand American adults, 69 percent had less than a thousand dollars in savings.

Many Americans are shocked at how little they have in savings when they reach the age of sixty-five. For some, that may have been because spending in the present outweighed concern over financial security in their senior years.

But we can remind ourselves that our actions *can* be controlled. At one large company, the rate of people who participated in 401(k) retirement savings plans was 40 percent when enrollment was optional, and opt in, whereas enrollment rates went up to 90 percent when the company changed to automatic enrollment, and made it necessary to take certain steps to opt out. It means that it's possible to improve major issues like retirement funds simply by lowering the hurdle for enrollment and raising the hurdle for withdrawal.

## Applying habits to interpersonal relationships

Habits can also be employed to improve interpersonal relationships. If you see that you're about to run out of toilet paper (a trigger), you can replace it without waiting for the next person (routine), and you can feel that you're promptly handling housework (reward).

Acquire a habit like that, and you won't have useless arguments with your roommate.

One tip for acquiring habits, to set a date, is particularly effective in various social situations. We've been having class reunions at my junior high school for more than fifteen years, which I think is possible because the date is always set for December 30. Because we know that it's being held on this day every year, we're aware of it ahead of time and make the necessary plans and adjustments, and the participation rate is high.

It's also an effective strategy for friendships. Two close friends and I would usually only get together on each of our birthdays. It was easy to work out because the dates were set, and the habit of getting together went on for many years.

Strategies for acquiring habits can also be applied to romantic relationships. It's often said that detail-oriented guys are popular with women. Women might appreciate—and start to expect—being frequently praised and told that their man loves them. Do take note, though, that there may be cases where a woman gets seriously annoyed.

It's also possible to use your knowledge of habits to deal with annoying people. Although you may be annoyed, you might also feel sympathy towards the person, and continue to respond when they contact you. But by doing that, the person will continue to expect the reward, and make it a habit to keep talking to you. It's sometimes effective to clearly set boundaries.

# Step 48: Create habits that are unique to you

> *It were not best that we should all think alike; it is differ-*
> *ence of opinion that makes horse races.*
>
> —Mark Twain

Ichiro has reflected on the intensive training he used to go through like this:

"It's true that when I was spending time at the Orix training camp when I was eighteen, nineteen and twenty, I was hitting hundreds of balls until two or three in the morning. Looking back, I can see that it wasn't a rational way to practice. But if someone told me that at the time and I hadn't done it, thinking that it was a waste of time, I wonder if I would have thought this way now."

I want to convey the same idea with this book. I didn't decide to quit drinking because I understood the disadvantages of drinking; it was because I had personally accumulated a lot of experiences of regret. A person who doesn't have that degree of regret probably wouldn't come up with the idea of quitting drinking. I decided that I had to seriously acquire good habits because my own experiences of slacking off showed me that it wasn't good to live like that.

I don't think that what I write in this book will be applied exactly as written by readers. I hope you'll acquire original methodologies of your own as you go through the process of trial and error.

When you set out to learn from a book, you want to read about the common pitfalls before you begin. But you won't understand the pain of a pitfall unless you actually fall. It's because of that pain that you'll try not to fall next time. I know I can't warn you about all the pitfalls in advance. But there are some you'll keep falling into, even if you're cautious, and I want to make you aware of those.

## I'd like you to create original habits

Although I used to think that I was a night person, I was able to switch to being a morning person. And I can now start the day off feeling good. I think that particular example is general enough to apply to other people as well, and I'd like to recommend it to anyone who is interested.

But Masashi Ueda, whose four-panel newspaper comic strip, *Kobo, the Li'l Rascal*, has been running for a long time, leads a completely different lifestyle. He goes to bed at three-thirty in the morning and wakes up at ten-thirty. That's because a bike courier comes to pick up his daily manuscripts at three-thirty, and counting backwards from that deadline, he says it's best for him to get up at ten-thirty.

It's this sense of something being "the best for oneself" that's important. It's true that I might be happy if someone copied my habits. But we all live in different places, we're different ages, and we're different genders. It's useless to suggest to a sumo wrestler that he go on a diet. The situation will vary from person to person, and I hope that you will create a customized method that's right for you.

There are also things that seem necessary for all of us despite our different situations. Records are one example. You should keep records of the conditions—your mood, physical condition, the season, how busy you are—in which you can or can't continue to practice your habits. If you keep records, you'll begin to see how to avoid difficulties that you've experienced before. It would make me happy if you could read between the lines in this book and take away that kind of understanding. There are no examples of habits that you *have* to acquire. The important thing is to think for yourself.

# Step 49: Make peace with the knowledge that your habits will eventually collapse

*Habits are surprisingly tough, and habits are surprisingly fragile.*

—Gretchen Rubin

Meditation is the act of returning our awareness back to our breathing after it starts to wander, but our awareness keeps flying off somewhere no matter how we continue to bring it back. The Buddhist monk Ryunosuke Koike expressed the phenomenon like this: "It's like being shaken off when you try to ride a horse but you continue to try to get back on the horse no matter how many times you're shaken off."

Meditation is something you should make into a habit, but I think this expression describes habits in general. No matter how you approach making something into a habit, you'll continue to be shaken off. Habits will eventually collapse. The important thing is to keep rebuilding them.

## Write a "spell of restoration"

You might have to abandon your normal routines for a brief period, or sustain an injury during a trip that prevents you from doing things as usual, and you'll find that the habits you've developed will collapse in a few days or weeks.

One countermeasure for such an occurrence is to write detailed notes on what it's like when particular habits are going well—what it's like when you're in a state of flow. For me, that's the timetable I mentioned at the beginning of this book. When we keep notes on the methods that have worked, we become confident that we can always find our way back to that state.

We also forget things about ourselves sometimes, but we can take notes so that later we'll be able to remember. We can start over if we have things written down. It's like our very own "spell of restoration," used in the place of saving data in the game *Dragon Quest II.* We can write these types of notes ourselves.

It's true that some things can't be dealt with using a "spell of restoration." If you move, change jobs, get married, or have a baby, you have no choice but to change the habits that you had that were linked to your previous conditions.

But even after that type of life-changing event, I think these methods for acquiring habits still apply: you may need to acquire new habits, like getting up early in the morning for your kids, taking them to school, or taking your family's new dog out for a walk.

It isn't just your conditions; you, too, will gradually change. Of course, you'll get older. There's no need to read a book on biology to see that we're a little different today than we were yesterday. So to make our habits match who we are, we need to continue to make adjustments.

## Maintain a sense of novelty in achieving habits

The author Nicholson Baker structures his work using habits, and says he tries a somewhat different approach whenever he writes a new book. For example, "from now on, I'm only going to write on the back porch in flip flops starting at four o'clock in the afternoon." That way, he maintains a sense of novelty. The habits of mine that I've written about here are only for the time being. You have to continue to make changes and slight adjustments so that you don't get bored.

Here's some advice from Daigo Umehara about making changes: "When you want to make a change to yourself, a tip is to not think about whether it will make things better. If things get bad, you can make another change when you realize it." If a change doesn't change things the way you wanted it to, you can make another change.

Committing to the practice of acquiring habits is different from being stubborn with the specific habits that you've formed.

# Step 50: Know that there is no end to habits

*As long as you live, keep learning how to live.*

—Seneca

One thing I used to misunderstand about minimalists: I thought the process of becoming a minimalist "ended" at some point.

When I let go of things I didn't need, I thought to myself, "Now I'll be free from my concerns over my things."

I thought it would be easy if only I could find clothes that I would want to wear my entire life like Steve Jobs: "All I have to do is wear a white shirt all my life. It's super-convenient!" But after moving from Tokyo to the countryside, I've had barely any opportunities to wear white shirts, since they get soiled easily.

And new things become necessary, while others I have to get rid of, depending on my interests. It's because I've realized that my journey as a minimalist hasn't come to an end that I can once again feel joy in letting things go.

At the moment, there are no more habits that I want to acquire. But that doesn't mean I've finished acquiring habits. Because even if I'm able to develop my current habits, there will be new, tougher habits that I'll want to take on.

## The very act of continuing to form habits is a habit

Even when there are no issues at hand, people's minds will find a way to bring on challenges.

We're sad beings, who continue to find some kind of dissatisfaction or challenge—in what would look to anyone else like a peaceful life—which we must continue to overcome. But there are rewards in overcoming those challenges, and there is no end to those challenges. Isn't that actually something to be happy about?

Having acquired habits doesn't mean we're finished with our habits.

There is no end to habits.

It's a habit to continue to form habits.

CHAPTER 4

# WE'RE MADE OF HABITS

## We start to understand our "efforts" through our habits

I recall my father saying to our pet cat now and then, "You're lucky." It's true that there are times when you can feel envious of a cat who's always dozing and living a relaxed life. A bird is able to sing and do a mating dance without instruction, but we humans have to make an effort to learn to play an instrument or learn how to dance. Why is it that human beings are the only ones who have to make an effort?

I used to view life as a contest for enduring pain. Only those who have endured the pain of exerting themselves are the winners. But from what I've learned about habits to date, the reality of effort seems to be something completely different.

In this book, we've looked at the following in detail:

Chapter 1: When it is that people generate or lose willpower;

Chapter 2: That there are rewards to be found in actions that appear painful to others;

Chapter 3: Specific methods and concepts to help turn those actions into habits.

After giving this much thought to habits, we've already obtained clues about the true meaning of "effort" and "talent." Though we can't unveil everything, I think it's possible to sketch a basic outline. And it seems that effort and talent work differently from how people generally think they do.

## Does Ichiro make an effort?

Let us first think about effort. In the Japanese expression "effort will make you bleed," the word "effort" is associated with pain. Is that true?

Since childhood, Ichiro has been practicing baseball more than anyone else. In an essay written in his final year of elementary school, he claimed, "I have tough practices at least three hundred and sixty days out of three hundred and sixty-five." When he played for Orix, he did batting practice for two to three hours at a time. Other players would have wrapped up in twenty to thirty minutes. Coach Akira Ohgi watched Ichiro practicing diligently and said, "Of course he can hit if he practices that much. Though normal players can't practice like that."

During his days playing professional baseball, Ichiro was usually the first player on the field, warming up and practicing, even on his off days. Ichiro was always there at practice, regardless of whether he was playing in a game. Any way you look at it, it sounds like hard work, but Ichiro always says: "I don't make an effort."

## Haruki Murakami's efforts aren't much?

As mentioned before, when working on long novels, Haruki Murakami writes ten pages every day and never misses his hour of running or swimming.

But even Murakami said in an interview: "In short, whether it's work or something else, I'm just doing what I like to do, the way I like to do it. It isn't like being stoic or anything. I do hardly anything that I don't want to do. Making a little effort in something you enjoy doing, that's not a big deal."

People who appear to be making constant, Herculean efforts deny that they are doing so, or claim that it's no big deal. For a long time, I thought that such words were expressions of modesty typical of top athletes and writers. Of course, we can't easily imagine the type of effort they make, but I think I've gained a little understanding of what they mean.

The confusion is probably caused by the fact that the word "effort" is used with two meanings.

## Separating effort from endurance

The two meanings contained in the word "effort"—it's my belief that it's better to separate these into the conventional meanings of "effort" versus "endurance."

I see the difference between them in the following way:

"Effort" brings you a steady reward that compensates you for the price you pay.

"Endurance" is on display when you don't have a legitimate reward for the price you pay.

"Endurance" is often encouraged in Japanese society. For example, working at a company means receiving a "reward" called a salary. In order to receive that reward, people pay various prices—including time. Other payments can be required as well, depending on the company:

- You can't decide when to report to work or leave the office.

- You can't ignore bosses that you don't like, clients, or customers.
- It's hard to take time off, even if you're tired or you have to take care of your kids.
- You don't have the discretion to make decisions; you only do what you're told to do.

Of course, there are other possible forms of reward besides a salary:

- Praise for your work from colleagues and superiors.
- A sense of unity when you accomplish your work as a team.
- The sense that your work is helping someone.

If you're going to work every day when you don't want to, that's already in the realm of "endurance." But if compensation is commensurate with payment, you'll go ahead and do it. People don't want to do things if what they're paying is greater than what they're receiving.

## Whether it's your choice

Besides, whether or not the reward that you receive matches what you're paying, a key point in determining whether something takes effort or endurance is whether you're making the choice yourself.

In the radish test, the students who could only eat radishes appeared to lose willpower. But we can also look at it this way: they were told, "You can *only* eat the radishes," even though there were chocolate chip cookies in front of them, too.

If you *choose* to eat the radishes, rather than being forced to, your willpower will not be decreased.

First of all, it's stressful to be forbidden from doing something, or to be ordered around without a choice.

Here's another experiment: two rats placed in separate cages are—the poor things—given an electric shock. Of the two rats, only one of them can press a lever that allows both to escape the electric shock. As a result, the rat without access to the lever ends up showing signs of chronic stress, which leads to weight loss, ulcers, and even a higher incidence rate of cancer. Although both rats are given the electric shock for the same amount of time, the rat with the power to choose to avoid the shock experiences less stress.

We can think of "effort" as the tolerance required to do what you want and choose to do, whereas "endurance" is tolerance in a situation where you haven't made a choice and are forced to do something that you don't want to do. We continue to practice our habits because these are actions that we have chosen to do. You can continue to do something if you like doing it, because regardless of the type of suffering it may entail, you have understood and made a choice.

## There are also stages of endurance in habits

Endurance is like being made to continue to climb a mountain with neither peak nor downhill paths, one that only continues to rise.

Effort isn't like that. Of course there are uphill climbs here and there, and those are painful, but you have a sense of achievement when you reach the summit, and it's refreshing to go downhill. There are rewards that match your effort.

When acquiring a habit, though, there is first a period resembling "endurance." There is a greater price to pay at the beginning; it feels like everything is a struggle, or it's tough on your body. That's why we often end up quitting after a few days or so.

I mentioned ways to overcome that period of endurance in Chapter 3. The "effort zone" awaits you when you overcome the period of endurance. Once you reach that, habits will no longer be acts that are merely painful, and you'll be able to receive many rewards.

## It's okay to judge your own efforts by your own standards

There will probably be times when someone else's efforts seem amazing. I sometimes wonder if I'm not making enough of an effort when I see someone biting their lip and letting out a weird cry as they lift a two-hundred-pound barbell.

But I believe that the effort made by the newcomer at the gym, attempting to lift a fifty-pound barbell without understanding

## The difference between effort and endurance

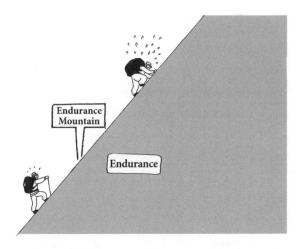

"Endurance" is only an upward climb with no rewards to match the price you've paid.

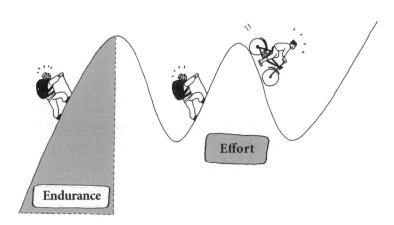

"Effort" brings rewards, like the sense of accomplishment in standing at the summit or the refreshing feeling of the descent. However, there is a stage of "endurance" before something becomes a habit.

what's what just yet, exceeds the effort made by a gym regular lift-ing a two-hundred-pound barbell. An easy standard to measure the level of effort is heart rate.

Here's an anecdote I love about heart rates, introduced in *Spark: The Revolutionary New Science of Exercise and the Brain*:

Phil Lawler, a junior high school PE teacher, added heart rates to the measurements taken during PE class. One day, he had an eleven-year-old girl who wasn't good at exercising put on a heart rate monitor as she ran. Since she wasn't good at exercising, her time probably wasn't good. But Lawler was surprised when he looked at her heart rate. In theory, a person's age is subtracted from 220 to get what is generally considered the maximum heart rate. And Lawler couldn't believe his eyes when he saw her heart rate: an average of 187.

Age eleven meant her maximum heart rate would be about 209. And it increased to 207 when she reached the finish line. That meant she had run mostly at full speed. Reflecting on that day, Lawler said:

"You gotta be kidding me! Normally, I would have gone to that girl and said, 'You need to get your ass in gear, little lady!'

"I started thinking back to all the kids we must have turned off to exercise because we weren't able to give them credit. I didn't have an athlete in class who knew how to work as hard as that little girl."

Running at a fast speed is different from doing your best. Whenever I read this anecdote, the tears start to fall. The girl who wasn't good at exercising had practically been crushing her chest putting in more of an effort than anyone else in her class.

## Talent interpreted through habits

*A professional writer is an amateur who didn't quit.*
—Richard Bach

Through learning about habits, my idea of what we call "talent" has also changed. I, too, used to think that talent was something that you were given in advance. I thought it was tied closely with genes and distributed at birth, and that some people have it while others don't. I used to feel that I, too, had been born as someone who didn't have it, and believed that it was really unfair.

But I wonder why that belief is so common. Successful people are sometimes said to have no natural talent, and they sometimes declare so themselves.

## Don't geniuses have talent?

Naoko Takahshi was the women's marathon gold medalist at the Sydney Olympics. Yoshio Koide, Takahashi's instructor, reportedly always told her: "You don't have talent. That's why you have to train the hardest in the world."

You'd think that no matter how you look at it, you need talent to be a gold medalist, right? Kyohei Sakaguchi, an author I mentioned earlier, puts it like this: "Some people say to me, 'You have talent; others are different,' but ten years ago, they said, 'You don't have talent, so you should quit.' Isn't perseverance amazing?"

Haruki Murakami also thought, until age twenty-nine, that

he'd be content living a quiet life and enjoying casual pastimes. All was fine as long as he could read, listen to music, and own a cat. He said in an interview, "I didn't even think at the time that I might be able to do something creative. I didn't think I had that type of talent."

## Were Einstein and Darwin just ordinary people?

Geniuses always say, "I'm ordinary." Charles Darwin lamented in his autobiography that he didn't have the capacity for intuitive understanding or memory.

Einstein also said that he wasn't particularly smart; he simply tackled problems for longer periods. If Darwin and Einstein weren't geniuses, then who is?

Darwin said that if he was better than ordinary people by any measure, it would be his ceaseless passion for natural science. This is Einstein's reasoning: "I have no special talents. I am only passionately curious."

Neither considered themselves particularly capable. But both possessed inexhaustible passion. That's why they were able to tackle tough problems for long periods. In other words, simply continuing was more important for their success than capability.

Isn't talent, then, something not distributed at birth, but rather grown from something that wasn't there to begin with?

## Talent isn't rare

Anson Dorrance is a soccer coach with the greatest number of wins in the history of US women's soccer. He's achieved twenty-two national victories in thirty-one years, and he says talent isn't something that's rare; whether or not you can become a great athlete depends on the effort you're willing to make to develop your talent.

The reason his teams achieve glorious results isn't his ability to identify and recruit only people with talent; instead, he makes the players who join his team work hard.

## The simple truth about talent

> *The vision of a champion is someone who is bent over, drenched in sweat, at the point of exhaustion when nobody else is watching.*
>
> —Anson Dorrance

Earlier, I introduced conclusions drawn by the sociologist Daniel Chambliss, who studied top swimmers for many years. These are the findings in one of his papers:

- The best performance is the result of accumulating countless small skills.
- There is nothing special or superhuman about what the athletes do.

- Athletes achieve outstanding results through continuous effort.

What this paper says is terribly ordinary: the ones who keep working diligently come out ahead. In fact, this conclusion seemed so ordinary that it wasn't well-received by his colleagues.

People expect more provocative arguments, like "Genes decide everything!" or "Your early education determines whether you become a genius!" But the truth is simple: the diligent continuation of habits creates talent.

The reason why geniuses say they don't have talent, or that they're ordinary, is that the procedures they follow are so very straightforward.

## Setting yourself apart from geniuses

> *Genius is a convenient word. If you say genius, people will probably think you've been managing with just the talent you were born with, without even making an effort.*
>
> —Ai Fukuhara

It's always stories about geniuses that we admire. The perfect performances put on by figure skater Yuzuru Hanyu and gymnast Kohei Uchimura once every four years make them look like geniuses of another dimension, and we like getting excited by their splendor, becoming enraptured, feeling a sense of unity with them.

Angela Duckworth introduces concepts, like the following

from Nietzsche, that explain such a tendency: When we see something that's too perfect, we don't think, "How can we be like that?" It's because there's no need to feel inferior in comparison when you think of a genius as a divine existence. "That person is superhuman" means "it's useless to compete."

In this way, words like "talent" and "genius" aren't used to praise someone, but are instead used to separate them from us.

When we see capacities that we can't compete with, rather than considering talent an extension of the efforts that we make, there's more relief in believing that it was generated at a place beyond our reach.

## The talent to add, and the talent to multiply

If the question becomes whether it's possible for *anyone* to become a genius, as long as they continue to make an effort, then I have to say that that certainly isn't the case.

In the same way that we differentiated between "effort" and "endurance," I would also like to differentiate between "talent" and "knack," which is contained in the term "talent."

The poet Machi Tawara says there's a "talent for adding" and a "talent for multiplying." Even if people start with the same level of experience, there are those who can only build their skills through addition and those who can quickly multiply their skills to achieve even greater results.

The difference here is what I would like to call a "knack." This is the distinction between knack and talent:

- Knack: A natural ability or predisposition for a certain skill, which helps you to acquire it quickly.
- Talent: The skills and capacities that you acquire as a result of continuing to do something.

For example, there are people who can quickly learn a foreign language, and we can say that they have a knack for it. When you have a knack for something, there is a rapid rate of skill development compared to the amount of effort that you make. But even if you don't have a knack for something, shouldn't it be possible to eventually arrive at the same skills and capacities, or "talent," with addition, if you continue to make an effort without giving up?

> *There are many who have become proud poets because they have been devoted to polishing what were far inferior talents in themselves.*
> —*Sangetsuki* ("The Moon Over the Mountain")

What we have at the outset are only small variations in our knacks. Let's say that there is a child who quickly picks up the tips during drawing class, and is praised, "You're good at drawing."

Because there's a reward—receiving praise—when a good picture is produced, the child will be happy and continue to draw. He'll doodle in his notebook during class. A sense of self-efficacy—"I can do it!"—will be generated, and he might show hand-drawn manga serials to his classmates. He'll receive even more praise and continue to draw even more. Because he draws often, his skills will get better and better.

The child might eventually want to apply to attend an art school. But he'll be shocked to learn that there are many people in the world who can draw just as well as he can, if not better. Among that multitude of talent, he'll likely receive less and less praise for his drawings, which will mean less reward, and that may lead to less motivation to draw. The less practice he gets, the less improvement there will be, which can lead to the line, "Oh, gee, I guess I didn't have talent."

Even if you can only build talent by addition, your skills will accumulate, as long as you continue to make an effort. But when you see the speed with which someone who has more of a knack than you do accumulates their skills, you may think that what you're doing is silly, and quit. Isn't this more a case of your skill development halting simply because you stopped working at it, rather than a lack of talent?

## To give up is to make something clear

> *God, grant me the serenity to accept the things I cannot change, courage to change the things I can, and wisdom to know the difference.*
>
> —Reinhold Niebuhr

Of course, it isn't as if everyone can become a professional or first-rate. There's always a limit, somewhere along the way. As William James said, "trees don't grow into the sky."

It's said that Dai Tamesue wanted to win a medal in the one-hundred-meter run, but switched to the four-hundred-meter hurdles after considering his physical condition. There are things that you can't change, like the fact that you weren't born in Jamaica or that you're not two meters tall. So Tamesue gave up the hundred meters. But he says that giving up is "making something clear." He didn't just walk away; he made clear what his limitations were.

## Being convinced, even if you get sick

That's what I want to do: learn my limits, and learn my prospects. To gracefully give up, or make those clear. I want to expose my limits and be truly satisfied with them.

Illness might be a straightforward example. At present, I get plenty of sleep, cook three meals a day, consume brown rice and vegetables, and exercise every day. I don't drink, and I don't smoke. I would get straight As in a medical interview sheet, and there's nothing else for me to do in watching my health.

Still, I may get sick someday. I think I'll be able to willingly accept it then—because I've done everything that I could. Illness would become one of my limitations, and I think I'd be able to concede to it.

## You can forget about a word like "talent"

This is where I recall words by Sō Takei: "Talking about someone's talent can wait until you've exceeded the effort that that person has made." A young child tries to button his shirt several times, but can't do it. What would happen if he then started to think, "I have no talent to button my shirt"? What if he saw an adult handling the series of actions that make up a normal morning routine and thought, "He's a genius"?

We similarly use the word "talent" as an excuse to give up on challenges for which we have no way to know how far we'll be able to go, way before we've actually reached our limit. We say we "don't have talent," and that's why we're giving up.

There are differences in our knacks, and there must also be differences in our limits. But that's something we can think about much later, after we've continued to work on our habits. There should be no need at all to talk about talent in our daily lives.

## How about genes?

Talent isn't something that we're given, it's something that's created as a result of continuation. But aren't the genes that we inherit from our parents involved? Of course they do have an impact.

As an example, the relatives of the musician Kenji Ozawa are tremendously impressive. Ozawa himself graduated from the University of Tokyo, his father is a scholar of German literature, his mother's a psychologist, the conductor Seiji Ozawa is his uncle, and many of his other relatives are also famous people. When we see an example like that, it looks like he was born in a class of his own to begin with, and naturally, that's partly true.

But if your relatives include a professional in a certain field, there should be less objection, within your family, for you to go into that area yourself, compared to other families. It should also impact your sense of self-efficacy to know that if your relatives are skilled in that area, you should he able to do it as well. How are we supposed to measure that kind of impact with genetic testing?

## The answer to "genes or environment?"

> *My advice to other disabled people would be, concentrate on things your disability doesn't prevent you doing well, and don't regret the things it interferes with.*
>
> —Stephen Hawking

Is it genetics that makes a person, or is it the environment? A consensus is starting to emerge for this long-debated, complicated issue.

Canadian psychologist Donald Hebb has answered that asking that question "is like saying that the area of the field depends more on its length than on its width." And my favorite response is what Walter Mischel said:

"Who we are emerges from a tightly intertwined dance between our environment and our genes that simply can't be reduced to either part alone."

## It's more effective to think potential is infinite

Snoopy said: "You play with the cards you're dealt." Cards that you're dealt include your knacks and your genes. But through habits, it should be possible to exchange some of your cards, like in a game of poker.

Psychologist Carol Dweck has ascertained something important. In a test on willpower, people who thought willpower was without limit did better than those who believed that it would decrease if you used it to complete a task. Putting aside whether or not willpower really does decrease, it was more effective to think that it didn't decrease.

I think the issue of talent and genetics is exactly the same. At the very least, there's no doubt that people who believe there's a lot of room for change can reach farther than those who think that most everything is determined by genes.

## Is it simply that I have a high level of self-awareness?

In practicing my habits, there was a time when I wondered if I simply had a high level of self-awareness about what I was doing. A friend of mine saw me give up liquor and sweets and said, "Your lifestyle ain't for me."

The psychologist Barry Schwartz divided people into two types: Those who are satisfied with the radio station that they're listening to now, and those who continue to change stations looking for something that'll satisfy them.

The former are "fairly satisfied"; they can be satisfied in their shopping if they find appropriate clothes. The latter are "perfectionists" who look for the very best outfit, and they have trouble buying clothes.

I think I fall completely under the latter category. Perfectionists feel joy if they find something that will satisfy them, but the psychological and physical price they pay for finding that "something" is high. When in full pursuit of an objective, one's happiness can be completely neglected.

I get depressed right away when I can't practice my habits. People who are like that can be said to have high expectations for themselves.

There are those who appear happy, even when they don't seem to excel at anything in particular. There are those who always wear a happy smile on their faces. I really think that talent and happiness are completely unrelated. It's my belief that you don't need to tell people who are already happy to acquire good habits or to make more of an effort.

## The greatest reward is the ability to like yourself

> *Don't ask yourself what the world needs. Ask yourself what makes you come alive and then go do that. Because what the world needs is people who have come alive.*
> —Howard Thurman

There are words said by a young actress that I can't forget: "I can like myself when I hustle." While various rewards may be obtained by successfully acquiring a habit, I think the maximum reward is a sense of self-approval, to be able to like yourself.

One day, I was looking at Twitter and something jumped out at me—a tweet from @eraitencho: "Isn't a goal that's effective for most people 'to become a person in a good mood'?"

I'm basically a person who is frighteningly laid-back, but I still get excited when I've accomplished all my daily habits. I can get in a good mood when I have the sense that I've done the things that should have been done today.

When things go well and I'm in a good mood, I can cheer on

other people as they make their own efforts. When things aren't going well, I want to take it out on others. When I'm absorbed in whatever I want to do, it doesn't bother me much what others do; it's like I don't have time to deal with it.

But people who can't do what they want to do and think they're a failure will tend to want to say that the results from someone else's efforts aren't much. When you haven't made an effort, you often want to downplay the efforts that someone else has made. I think this is a natural defensive reaction.

Unproductive criticism like that often stems from self-doubt. The truth looks distorted if you're teary-eyed. We should try to stay in a good mood to the extent that we can, and be nice to people.

## It isn't as if everyone aims to become the best of the best

Anders Ericsson, who has studied top athletes, musicians, and academics, says there isn't a single person among the crème de la crème who claims that practice is fun. For example, an initiative is under way among marathon runners to run under two hours. It's really tough to compete in something like the marathon, where people battle over something as clear-cut as times. The challenge is nothing less than trying to run faster than anyone else in the human race who has lived to date, and it requires efforts beyond the imagination.

Training that pushes you well outside your comfort zone and exceeds previous human limits can't be easy. What we aim for doesn't have to be like that. I feel that every person has a "judge" within them.

You could say that I have a fairly strict judge, because I feel bad when I can't acquire a habit that I set out to acquire. But even if I can't get up early or I can't exercise, I can let myself say, "Oh, well, it's okay," and be in a good mood.

I saw a friend from high school who was very fat. He laughed about it, saying, "But I thought, it's okay now." He had accomplished giving up, that is, he made his limitations clear. Though I'm not aiming to achieve the same state, we all need conviction, like my friend.

## Are habits simply primitive living?

> *For the simplicity that lies this side of complexity, I would not give a fig, but for the simplicity that lies on the other side of complexity, I would give my life.*
> —Oliver Wendell Holmes

The words above make me want to stop and say, hey, wait a minute. The habits I'm now practicing, when you get right down to it, are all very simple. The psychiatrist John Ratey says, "I think the best advice is to follow our ancestors' routine."

This is how our ancestors' routine went: They woke when the sun rose, and went to sleep when the sun set. They were mobile, hunting or gathering food—work, exercise—for periods that weren't too long, received teachings from nature and from their elders—learning—and they sang and danced—hobbies, arts.

The human body is equipped with a framework that's optimal for these types of actions. It becomes easy for the neurons for learning to develop when we exercise and stress hormones are released, sometimes so much so that we feel euphoric when there is pain from exercise, as we've seen several times in this book.

But when transportation systems become as developed as they are today, we don't need to exercise, and there are times when our bodies don't move because we've eaten too much good food. Then it becomes tough to experience the joys that we were initially equipped for.

Buying a car, enjoying a trip, going to a good restaurant, making sure our children receive a good education. The costs of living today are enormous. We then have to sacrifice our precious sleep, and work to earn money to pay those costs. In a way we misplace our priorities.

I think that after taking detour after detour, I have obtained, through my habits, the joy that I should have been able to feel naturally simply by living.

## An era when living tied into development

I feel that, in the past, life might have been full of a sense of joy as development progressed. That was possible because people hadn't yet broken down their work into specialized fields.

It wasn't only the techniques to track and catch our prey that we had to learn in the past. We predicted the weather from our environment, looked for water, wove ropes, and made utensils. We used our ideas to build houses from natural materials. We would draw, and we would tell our fortunes. There must have been many surprises that we couldn't learn in a single lifetime.

Even if we don't go back to the days when people hunted, things were more or less like that until just before World War II, when most people began to work as company employees. *Hyakusho* (the Japanese word for "farmer") means a person who can do *hyaku* (a hundred) jobs. The longer a person lived, the more things there were to learn, so it was natural to respect elders. Living was directly connected to development until that time.

## Why do people seek development?

According to athlete, artist, and author Gregory Burns, a large amount of dopamine is released when we encounter something unexpected or when we take actions we've never taken before—in other words, when we feel that something is new. Burns thinks that more than anything, this may be because obtaining new information about an environment helps survival.

The psychologist Robert W. White asserted the following: People try to gather information about their environment and thus enhance their ability to work in that environment, and people also have an instinct to reflect on and test what they can do for the environment.

People who've been thrilled by watching Nasu-D, a television producer known for his traveling adventures, and who have dreamed of drifting away to a deserted island, as in films like *Cast Away*, can probably well understand this instinct. White called this instinct "competence."

We probably would have been able to gain a thorough sense of this competence if it were ten thousand years ago when people were leading nomadic lives. If we changed houses periodically, we would have the joy of exploring our new environment each time, and there would also be the joy of gaining control over each new environment.

This instinct is probably what drives curiosity and the desire for self-development.

## An era when development needs to be sought intentionally

I feel that unlike our ancestors, people today have to seek opportunities for development intentionally.

I'll give you some examples from my own life. As I learned about wild grasses that were edible, I began to look seriously at the grass that grew on the side of the road, and the scenery changed. When I take part in a workshop on plastering or flooring work, I find that I'm interested in renovation methods for stores, and when I took up architecture, hoping to build my own mobile home, I began to look at temples in a different light. After experiencing rafting in a rubber boat, I would ask myself, "How could you go down that river?" whenever I saw a river from my car window.

You begin to see the world differently. Once upon a time, people used to be able to identify edible grass, structures, ways to cross a river, and so forth through their everyday experiences. Because there's no longer a need to do things like that today, we have to make a conscious effort to look for opportunities to hone our inquisitiveness.

This is how I think of moving my body. The more I practice yoga, the more I'm able to hear what my body has to say. The more I run, the closer I get to my body.

If we don't cultivate our own opportunities for development, we'll only be able to find joy in modern society's "ready-made" fun. Amusement parks and smartphone games are fun, too—it's because they're designed so that anyone can enjoy them. But activities structured so that we have to "Enjoy this in this way!"—where the way to have fun is already decided—will eventually bore us. And then, someday, we'll be bored with ourselves.

Making it a habit to seek unique opportunities for development, and gaining the sense that we're always doing something "new": these are things that satisfy human instinct.

## There's a hole in the wallet of happiness

> *Don't be caught up with success! Be caught up with development.*
>
> —Keisuke Honda

There are also other reasons why I feel that constant self-development is necessary. This thing called happiness isn't something that can be saved up. There's a big hole in the bottom of a wallet of happiness.

I told you earlier about Olympic athletes who became depressed, and Apollo astronauts being hit with similar symptoms. Although the scale is completely different, I think I had a similar experience, too. My previous work, *Goodbye, Things*, sold really well, and it was translated into more than twenty languages. Reprints were continuously issued, and I think hundreds of media outlets in Japan and abroad covered it. I'm still grateful to receive emails from overseas saying, "My life has changed."

Seen from the outside, this is a major success. It's more than enough of an achievement for a previously completely unknown individual to have accomplished. But accomplishing something became no more than a single reference point in the blink of an eye.

After continuing to say the same thing over and over again at interviews, I had a sense that I was fading away. When I go back and read my diary, I find that I frequently tormented myself immediately after my book sold and I succeeded. I drank too much and got depressed, and kept feeling down about the fact that I could no longer feel something substantial from my work.

Happiness isn't like money; you can't dip into a "savings of happiness" that you put away in the past to make up for a sense of self-doubt today.

Willpower is affected by the actions you've just taken. When you've just accomplished something, a sense of self-approval is produced. So it's necessary to engineer a sense of satisfaction every day, and a sense of substantial development. You can't obtain a sense of self-approval by talking about past achievements.

## Your uncertainties won't go away, so deal with your uncertainties well

*Even if you gain experience, your uncertainties won't go away. The only way is to act together with your uncertainties.*
—Ren Osugi

Feeling a sense of self-approval every day through my habits, I became able to deal with my uncertainties well. A freelancer will tend to have uncertainties: "Will I keep finding work?" "How much do I have left in my savings?" But I no longer have uncertainties like that.

It wasn't when my savings decreased to such-and-such an amount that I was hit with uncertainty. It was at the end of a day when I wasn't able to do substantial work, and ended up slacking off. It wasn't objective concerns like the balance of my savings, but instead regrets I had that prompted the onset of uncertainty.

The same thing happened when I considered issues like weight. There were times that I would get plenty of exercise and keep myself in control, and the next day, I would see that I had gained weight. But I realized that I didn't feel down at all at times like that. It doesn't bother me, even if I don't get results, when I'm doing what I should be doing. What gets me down is when I know I'm not doing what I should be doing.

Uncertainties and worries are really an issue of moods. It isn't the problem in itself; it's about your mood, how you're looking at the problem. I run when I feel depressed. I improve the blood flow to my brain and get help from dopamine and cortisol. That way, I feel better, and I start to feel that I can resolve my problems in any way I want.

## Uncertainties are necessary

Pain is disagreeable, but it's an important sign. If you fracture your leg but can't feel the pain, you won't be able to guard the affected site, and it'll end up getting worse. The same goes for fatigue. It's a sign that a day has been fulfilling, and that we've accomplished something.

Uncertainty is also a sign. Without it, people would take reckless actions without thinking ahead. We create plans because of our uncertainty. Excessive uncertainty isn't a good thing, but having an adequate amount is a sign that you're well-positioned for self-development. I mentioned earlier that when you focus on acquiring habits, you no longer have time to worry. And when you have a daily sense of self-approval through your habits, you become able to deal well with the uncertainties that will never go away.

Uncertainties are what you feel towards the future. And what lies ahead after you continue to care for the now is the future. There is no way that the future, the result of the now in which you accumulate satisfaction every single day, can turn out badly.

## The mind is made of habits

*All that we are arises with our thoughts.*
*With our thoughts we make the world.*
            —*The Dhammapada: The Sayings of the Buddha*,
                        translated by Thomas Byrom

Now, it isn't only with actions that people often resolve to do at the start of a new year, like getting up early or exercising, that the structure of habits gets to work. Our minds are also made of habits. For example, the words that people say are often habits, in the sense that we say them without much thought.

When a preschool-age child gets off a bus, it warms our hearts to hear the child saying in a loud voice, "Thank you!" But somewhere along the way as we grow older, we stop saying words of appreciation.

Although we pay the fare, we won't be able to reach our destination without the bus driver's driving. It isn't as if the charge will increase if we express our feelings of gratitude. There should instead be an increase in the driver's pride in his work, his sense of self-efficacy, if we express our feelings of gratitude. Thus thinking, I decided to start saying "Thank you" whenever I get off a bus.

But even with something simple like that, I was on my guard at the start. My heart rate would go up when I pulled out my wallet to pay the fare; I knew that most of the other riders don't say "Thank you." But as I continued to do it again and again, the words of gratitude started to come out without particular thought whenever I got off the bus. It became a habit.

## Habits of smiles and kindness

When someone drops their handkerchief during their commute, I pick it up for them right away. It isn't an action that has to do with thought, it's a habit of kindness. What moved me when I went to New York was that everyone helped without a second thought when they saw a person with a heavy baby stroller. Kindness to strangers is a habit, like a reflex. In Japan, everyone may want to help, but they hesitate a little.

Let's remember that willpower isn't something that decreases when it's used, but rather something that is recovered with our emotions. A little kindness gives joy to both parties. After extending kindness, we should be able to better tackle the challenges in our own lives.

Some people have nice smiles—contagious smiles. I'm not good at smiling, and the mimetic muscles around my mouth used to be stiff. So I made it a habit to smile when I saw myself in my mirror at home. It may sound weird, but after doing it over and over, I was able to smile automatically, just by seeing a mirror. I'm still not good at showing a smile to other people. But after making it a habit, it's a little easier than it used to be when I'm having my picture taken. Something that you thought was your personality can change with a simple habit.

## The habit of thought

I used to think that I was really bad at public speaking, but I made up my mind to do it so that I could talk about minimalism, and I appeared on a lot of radio shows. Then, for some reason, the answers came smoothly no matter what I was asked.

It was no wonder, because I'd thought about minimalism for a long time, and while writing *Goodbye, Things* I had repeatedly asked myself questions I anticipated being asked. So for me, the questions were my trigger, and the answers I gave were a routine that I was already familiar with.

It probably isn't public speaking in and of itself that people aren't good at. Anyone, no matter how smart they are, would probably stammer if they were suddenly asked to comment on an issue that they'd never even thought about.

In these ways, we can say that the statements that suddenly come out of a person's mouth are shaped by their habits of thought. There are various thoughts that have become habits for me as a result of continuing to think about minimalism.

While the dominant value in the world today is that the more things you have, the better off you are, I've learned that you can have plenty with just a few things, I developed a habit of think-ing about the question, "Are the values believed in the world today true?"

I came to understand that you lose something if you obtain something, and you will gain something when you lose something. I started to ask myself, "What is the value of not having something?"

For example, maybe I see a family with kids who look happy during a picnic at the park, and they will sometimes look dazzling, even to me, though I don't have children. But the next moment, I remember the value of freedom, and the carefree life that I've been able to live.

You can start to automatically recognize the values that are important to you without having to inspect them each time. There's no way you'll forget what's important to you; you should simply put those values into practice every day. These are habits of thinking. The values you've chosen over and over again will eventually become habits. You'll be able to choose with barely any conscious thought.

The artist and writer Taro Okamoto's choices were always clear-cut as well: "Whatever is likely to fail." He always chose to take on tough challenges that looked like they would ruin his success.

You don't consciously worry about most choices; they're decided instantly by your habits. People don't have the capacity to consider every choice in detail and choose what's best. But regardless of the results, they can accept the choices that they've made if they're aligned with their own values.

What people *are* able to do is look back and believe that they made the best choice. People who know that make their decisions more quickly.

## Habits are being made this very moment

William James used the example of water hollowing out a channel for itself to describe the process of habit-making. Even if water tries to flow where there's no path yet, the flow will only spread out, since there are no good passages at the beginning.

But when water continues to flow again and again in the same direction, a channel is formed, and it gets deeper and wider. The flow of that water is exactly like the neural circuit. Electrical signs are sent to the neurons receiving stimulation, and the connection will become stronger with more flow.

There's a saying that goes, "A person will become exactly the type of person that he continues to think about all day." Each of the seventy thousand thoughts that a person has over the course of a day will be reflected inside him, and they will gradually make an impact.

God may be too busy to watch what you're doing. But your brain is being impacted this very moment by the things you're thinking and seeing, and it continues to create habits.

## The pain of slacking off, the pain of being active

> You do not use your brain to keep the stuff out. You use your brain to take it in.
> —Next Stop, Greenwich Village

During the six months I spent slacking off, there were certainly things that I enjoyed, but I experienced no joy of development or satisfaction, and it was painful.

You may see those who are unable to move or work and blame them, saying, "They're lazy." And when those people are pushed into a corner, you may think, "It's their responsibility." But I know that a state where you're being lazy or only having fun isn't truly joyful. It's a truly tough situation, in which there's no sense of self-approval or self-efficacy.

On the other hand, people who are active also go through pain. The rewards that they receive, like income and people's praise, may appear large. But there is pain behind the effort that they make, and they also feel a lot of pressure from their communities.

When asked if he would choose the same road if he were born again, Ichiro has said, "Never." From here on, this is my imagination at work: Even if you continue to produce results, people gradually start to take those results for granted when you're at the Ichiro level. It seems impossible that you'd ever become weak, even if you get older. This is Ichiro; he should be able to handle it. If the expectations grow large enough to themselves enter the Hall of Fame, then perhaps the rewards that someone like Ichiro can obtain will decrease.

## Happiness from an emotional standpoint

Willpower can't be fully trained, because it's linked with your emotions—and they're never totally under your control, no matter how far you go. You can see the proof of that when you look at how "first-rate" people act.

Professional athletes fall under the influence of drugs, become addicted to sex, or can't overcome the temptation of doping. It doesn't matter if they're politicians, film producers, or whatever; we should all keep in mind the scandals of successful people. Even Eric Clapton and Brad Pitt became dependent on alcohol, and Zinedine Zidane's retirement match ended with head-butting.

Bruno Mars, who won seven Grammy awards in 2018, came to Japan for the first time in four years and gave a live performance at Saitama Super Arena. And he got angry at audience members sitting in the front row who took pictures of themselves with their smartphones during the performance, and threw towels at them. No matter how successful he may have been, he was more unhappy at that moment than the people sitting in the area and laughing.

In this way, people are people, no matter how far they get. But we expect people who are outstanding and people who are in positions of responsibility to exercise their willpower 24/7. There's no one anywhere in the world who can do that. Willpower is linked with emotions, and there's no one who doesn't have emotions.

So we should see those outstanding people more as individual human beings, just like us. At minimum, it would be wrong to deny everything else that a person has achieved when he or she makes a mistake. Because no matter how successful someone becomes, there's still a foolish side to them that makes them that much more lovable.

## Everyone is happy to a fair degree and unhappy to a fair degree

> *It's only when we are otherwise engaged—you know, focused, absorbed, inspired, communicating, discovering, learning—dancing, for heaven's sake!—that we experience happiness as a by-product, a side effect. Oh, no, we should concern ourselves not so much with the pursuit of happiness, but with the happiness of pursuit.*
>
> *—Hector and the Search for Happiness*

A person can't continue to feed off the same joy from something they've already acquired. The evolutionary psychologist Daniel Nettle explains this human tendency like so: you may like a strawberry field fine, but there might also be some good salmon in the river over there.

A strawberry field is plenty to live off of, and it should be easy to maintain as long as you don't encounter unexpected challenges, but for some reason, people aren't satisfied with that. Here's the biological explanation: When you overestimate something that you already have (the strawberry field), you won't be able to survive when your environment changes. On the other hand, if you can find a replacement, you'll be able to survive, even if the original strawberry field becomes useless. So people are always looking for the next new thing.

People would be happier if they could be satisfied with what they have now, without becoming bored. But people are instinctively inclined to get bored of what they have now, and pursue new things. So no matter how successful they become, they will worry, and find reasons to feel uncertain—because people are geniuses at finding those. They will get used to any environment, and they'll get bored with it. Biologically, people prospered because of that instinct.

Worries, concerns: it's better to think of them not as personal issues but as a structure that people are born with. One of the musician Kenta Maeno's song titles goes like this: "Worries, concerns, fantastic!!" If we need to carry them with us forever, we might as well make them our friends.

When I wrote my previous book, I gained deep insights. I achieved fantastic success. But I had my next objective right away, and I can't help wanting to do well again. It'll be the same next time, and I guess the only way to keep going is to accumulate new successes. And I no longer think much about what happiness is.

Being able to sleep with peace of mind, having no shortage of food, and having friends and loved ones that you get along with: once a person fulfills those needs, they're fairly happy and fairly unhappy no matter how far they go.

## A partner called suffering

> *Suffering will not disappear. Things disappear when you suffer.*
>
> —Sochoku Nagai

When I first began to acquire habits, I thought about joy and suffering like this:

- First, you suffer, then you have fun = effort
- First, you have fun, and then you suffer = negligence

I used to wonder if the only difference between joy and suffering was the order, and if effort and negligence were mostly made up of the same actions.

And as I further continued to practice my habits, pleasure and pain became even harder to understand. Naturally, effort includes suffering. You get out of breath when you run, and your muscles will scream when you lift barbells. But once those actions are over, you gain a sense of satisfaction. As you continue to repeat those actions over and over, you begin to understand that it's *because* of the suffering that you now feel that sense of satisfaction.

When you continue to repeat those actions enough times, you'll become unable to tell whether it's suffering that you're feeling or if it's joy. Over time, you'll find that joy and suffering are like two sides of the same coin, or maybe they even overlap. You start to feel like the joy is apparent within the suffering, and you experience pleasure and pain simultaneously.

It isn't as if the suffering goes away after actions like running and weightlifting become habits. But you get used to the fact that suffering exists, and—how can I put it—the suffering starts to seem like a regular person who's always around.

I used to think that reducing the suffering as much as possible was a good thing, but it seems that that isn't the case. The Buddhist monk Sochoku Nagai says about training in Buddhism: When cleaning is part of the training, you're taught to thoroughly eliminate rationalizations such as, "This is already clean, so it doesn't have to be cleaned."

"As you're made to do things so much that it's 'Do this, do that,' and 'Yes, yes,' and you have no room to think, you eventually become able to concentrate, in each situation, on the thing you're supposed to do. Then, whether it's a gain or a loss, pleasure or pain, you start to make fewer decisions on your own. Eliminating the difference between loss and gain and between pleasure and pain is what is called 'attaining enlightenment.'"

I used to believe that you could compete with pain, win, and gain joy that exceeded it. But I'm starting to consider the pain in front of me from a different perspective. The English word "compete" comes from a Latin word the original meaning of which is said to be "to fight together." Like I'm in a gunfight in a crime film, I now have a feeling that I am relying on my partner by the name of pain, and I'm trusting that it has my back.

Suffering isn't the enemy. It's a partner with whom you fight.

## Running as I think, thinking as I run

I'm now dreaming of a scene.

I've always dreamed of running in a marathon, but for a long time, I'd simply been a spectator, thinking that all I could do was cheer after having seen the runners performing at a completely different level. I didn't try to run, either. All I did was read how-to books with titles like *How to Finish a Marathon*. I was scared to make a fool out of myself.

One day, I worked up the courage to take part in a marathon. But, yet again, I got caught up trying to get myself prepared. I should have heard the starting gun. But I was way too nervous to do that and kept tying my shoelaces over and over, and continued to engage in an extensive stretching routine.

Meanwhile, the other athletes had already started running. They were about to cross the finish line—and here I was, just having started my run.

I was pretty far behind. They could just as well start to pack up and leave by the time I reached the finish line. But this was where I finally realized that it didn't matter. No matter how far behind I may have been, whether or not I was able to finish the race within the designated time, it was okay. All was well, as long as I felt a sense of satisfaction. I wasn't in the spectator area, and I wasn't sitting at home in front of my TV. I was running right there on the marathon course just like the athletes.

Suffering: "It looks like things are gonna get tough now. Wanna quit?"

Me: "Hey, who do you think you're talking to?"

I'm going to tie my shoelaces, start to run, and see how things go.

# POSTSCRIPT

Writing this book was a major challenge. A challenge? God, I felt like I was stranded every day. Because it wasn't a habit for me to write my manuscript every day; that was the last habit that I acquired.

It says in my diary that on January 7, 2016, as I wrote while riding the train heading for Ochanomizu, I received a sign from heaven: "I'll write about habits as the theme for my next book!" Two and a half years passed before publication. Why did it take so long? I understand the reason now.

As John Updike put it—words I introduce in Step 32, "You can actually spend your whole life being a writer and totally do away with the writing." I had indeed gotten used to not writing, and "not writing" had become a habit. So I couldn't have written this book about habits without the knowledge about habits that I gained in the process. It's kind of weird: being taught by the content that I'm writing about as I became able to write about it.

Given that that was how the writing was going, I asked for an extension on the launch date on numerous occasions, and I did a super maneuver that only a former editor could do when I was way beyond the timing just before the final deadline. This was at the same time as the wedding and honeymoon of my editor Mai Yashiro, and I thought, "I have to get this done promptly before that and have her go on her trip feeling good!"—but it wasn't on time at all. Even under these conditions, her heartwarming personality helped me. Apologies from the bottom of my heart. And congratulations on your wedding.

Katsuya Uchida in the book publishing department read my manuscript and gave me sound advice when he wasn't even responsible for the project. I realized again how necessary it was for my writing to have as an editor someone who reads and offers his impressions. Thank you.

I was glad for the thoughtfulness of Yuki Aoyagi, chief editor of the book publishing department, shown to a rookie like me. Yes, this was published by Wani Books, where I previously worked. So I'm glad that I can see the faces of the people involved with this book. Toshiyuki Otsuka in the production department, Tokimasa Sakurai in the sales department, and everyone else, here I am causing trouble for you again.

I also extend my gratitude to Seiko Yamaguchi, for making illustrations that exceeded my expectations ("It would be nice if it came out like this . . ."), the designer Atsushi Nishitarumi for creating so many ideas for cover of the Japanese edition that it was tough to say which was best and for addressing my detailed requests.

I kept being a nuisance to the people in DTP, proofreading, and printing. I have to do things properly first, really. Serious reflection here. Thank you in advance to the people in distribution and handling, and at bookstores.

Everyone I touched on in this book: the researchers, creators, and athletes. Rather than saying that I wrote this book, it's like I went ahead and digested in my own way what you all said, edited it, and rearranged it. I earnestly admire your efforts.

Now, as I did in my last work, I want to thank my parents. This is what Walter Mischel of the marshmallow test, an integral theme in this book, has said about raising children: it wasn't children controlled excessively by their parents, but children whose choices and independence had been respected that obtained the skills necessary to be the most successful in the marshmallow test. Though I used to think that I was a person who had weak willpower, I think the fact that I was indeed raised by my parents in that way has somehow tied in to the habits that I've now acquired.

I began exercising when I was twenty-nine. I recently recalled that it was because of the influence of my father, who died that year, when he still had a long way to go. It seemed like he said to me, "Make sure you exercise properly and do things in moderation," and that was why I started exercising then. Oh, I was also influenced by my mother, who was a marathon runner! Thank you very much.

Now, one of the secrets to making something a habit is, as I said in Chapter 3, to advertise. That way, you put pressure on yourself. I think I, too, will reveal the topic of my next work. One, I'd like to write in more detail about quitting drinking, which I also touched on in this book. The working title is *Quit Alcohol in a Fun Way*. It's fun to drink alcohol, but it's also fun to quit drinking.

(Don't worry, I won't recommend it to people who don't want to quit.) I also want to write about the important topic of emotions, mixing it together with money and writing about something like "emotion-money theory." And that cognitive trick where people think of marshmallows as clouds. The title here would be *Go Ahead and Rewrite Reality as You Wish.*

Next time, I'd like to try various things, like running several projects at the same time. I'll get working on the next book as soon as I finish this manuscript, in the way of Anthony Trollope, the god of habits whom I love and respect (I haven't read his works though).

But jeez, my previous book, *Goodbye, Things* was translated a lot, so publishers abroad said things like, "We would love to translate a new work if it's by Fumio Sasaki!" The manuscript wasn't ready at all, and I thought it was just because of the pressure. But if I didn't want to answer to the expectations of people like that and readers who say, "I've ordered your book!" even before it goes on sale, I probably wouldn't be able to write books.

I'm clearly single, and I've retired to the countryside where I now live. I'll probably continue to live like this in the time to come. Even a guy like me couldn't write if it weren't for other people. I was able to affirm again that people live for people after all.

Fumio Sasaki
May 27, 2018

# RECAP

# THE 50 STEPS FOR ACQUIRING HABITS

1.  Sever ties with vicious circles.
2.  First, decide that you're going to quit.
3.  Leverage turning points.
4.  Quit completely—it's easier.
5.  Know that you always have to pay the price.
6.  Examine the triggers and rewards for your habits.
7.  Become a detective who looks for the real criminal.
8.  Don't make identity an excuse.
9.  Start with keystone habits.
10. Keep a diary to record observations about yourself.
11. Meditate to enhance your cognitive ability.
12. Realize that enthusiasm won't occur before you do something.
13. Whatever you do, lower your hurdles.
14. Realize that hurdles are more powerful than rewards.
15. Raise the hurdle for habits that you want to quit.
16. Spend money on your initial investment.

17. "Chunk down."

18. Make your targets ridiculously small.

19. Start today.

20. Do it every day (it's easier).

21. Don't make up "exceptions" as you go.

22. Enjoy it because you *aren't* good at it.

23. Set triggers.

24. Create an adult timetable.

25. Realize that no one has the power to concentrate.

26. Take action according to the date.

27. Set up a temporary reward.

28. Make good use of people's attention.

29. Make an advance declaration.

30. Think from a third-party perspective.

31. Quit in the middle of something.

32. Don't quit completely.

33. Keep records of your habits.

34. Take necessary breaks to conserve your strength.

35. Nap (the effects of a power nap are enormous).

36. Rest aggressively.

37. Cherish the things that you aren't making into habit.

38. Don't mix up your "objectives" and your "targets."

39. Look only at the targets in front of you.

40. Experience failures—they're indispensable for your habits.

41. Stop worrying about how long it will take for something to become a habit.

42. Do it; it's better than not doing it.

43. Gradually increase the level of difficulty.
44. Overcome each challenge along the way.
45. Keep at it, and increase your self-efficacy.
46. Create a chain reaction.
47. Adapt your habits as needed.
48. Create habits that are unique to you.
49. Make peace with the knowledge that your habits will eventually collapse.
50. Know that there is no end to habits.

# RECAP

# 14 GOOD HABIT INHIBITORS

1. Believing that a bad habit is necessary to relieve stress.
2. Trying to focus on just the good points.
3. Relying on your motivation.
4. Not having the right tools.
5. An awareness of the difficulties.
6. The sense of self-doubt produced by one failure.
7. Starting at a "good" time.
8. Thinking that tomorrow, you'll be Superman.
9. Creating an exception for the day in question.
10. Thinking that it's too late to start.
11. Not having a trigger.
12. Giving yourself a conflicting reward.
13. Pretending something never happened.
14. The "single-coin" issue.